FORENSIC RECOVERY OF HUMAN REMAINS

ARCHAEOLOGICAL APPROACHES

FORENSIC RECOVERY OF HUMAN REMAINS

ARCHAEOLOGICAL APPROACHES

TOSHA L. DUPRAS

JOHN J. SCHULTZ

SANDRA M. WHEELER

LANA J. WILLIAMS

CRC

Taylor & Francis
Taylor & Francis Group

Boca Raton   London   New York   Singapore

A CRC title, part of the Taylor & Francis imprint, a member of the
Taylor & Francis Group, the academic division of T&F Informa plc.

Published in 2006 by
CRC Press
Taylor & Francis Group
6000 Broken Sound Parkway NW, Suite 300
Boca Raton, FL 33487-2742

International Standard Book Number-10: 0-8493-2982-5 (Hardcover)
International Standard Book Number-13: 978-0-8493-2982-1 (Hardcover)
Library of Congress Card Number 2005043916

Library of Congress Cataloging-in-Publication Data

Forensic recovery of human remains : archaeological approaches / Tosha L. Dupras ... [et al.].
    p. cm.
Includes bibliographical references and index.
ISBN 0-8493-2982-5 (alk. paper)
1. Forensic anthropology. 2. Archaeology. 3. Human remains (Archaeology) 4. Criminal investigation. I. Dupras, Tosha L.

GN69.8F695 2005
614'.17--dc22   2005043916

Taylor & Francis Group
is the Academic Division of T&F Informa plc.

Visit the Taylor & Francis Web site at
http://www.taylorandfrancis.com

and the CRC Press Web site at
http://www.crcpress.com

Dedication

For my parents, Al and Neomee, and my brother Gene, who gave me the power to dream and the fortitude to follow those dreams. And to Valerio, for giving me unconditional love and support.

T.L.D

For Jana, every day is an adventure since you have been in my life.

J.J.S

For my mom, Michelina Wheeler, thanks for believing in us.

S.M.W

Also to Dr. Michael Spence for the many years of dedicated service to the victims and families involved in Ontario Provincial Police investigations.

L.J.W

Preface

Crime scenes involving human skeletal remains can be very complex scenes to process. Unfortunately, standard training for many crime scene units and law enforcement personnel typically does not include methods for search and recovery of human remains. Many investigators receive their first training at the time when human remains are found. Insufficient knowledge of archaeological techniques and skeletal biology can lead to crime scenes that are improperly processed, and vital evidence can be destroyed or overlooked. Certain skeletal elements may be missed because the individual performing the recovery does not have a framework for identifying or locating remains. Alternatively, individuals may be using search or excavation techniques that are unsuitable for the recovery of human remains. This book is intended to fill the need for an updated, comprehensive reference pertaining to, searching for, recovering, and excavating human remains and associated evidence (for example, botanical and entomological evidence) from forensic contexts.

The intended audience for this book is advanced undergraduates, graduate students, law enforcement and death scene personnel, forensic anthropology practitioners, and forensic archaeologists. In an ideal world, individuals with expertise in forensic anthropology and forensic archaeology would be present at every crime scene that involved the search for and recovery of human remains. However, we recognize that it is not possible in every situation for law enforcement agencies to call upon the expertise of a forensic anthropologist, forensic archaeologist, entomologist, or botanist. Because of this, our aim is to provide readers with information that will allow them to understand and use proper search, excavation, and recovery techniques as they apply to human remains.

This book describes techniques for use at less complicated scenes such as single burials. More complicated scenes, such as multiple or mass burials, water recoveries, or cremations, should be processed with the assistance of experienced personnel. Chapter 1 differentiates between forensic archaeology and forensic anthropology, and provides the reader with information on locating these specialists. Chapter 2 provides descriptions of the equipment necessary to conduct searches, recoveries, and excavations of human skeletal remains. Chapter 3 includes detailed information on how to conduct a search for skeletal remains deposited on the surface and for clandestine burials. Chapter 4 highlights different types of geophysical technologies that can be used for forensic searches. Chapter 5 focuses on the procedures for collecting associated botanical and entomological evidence at the scene. Chapter 6 describes various techniques for mapping and documenting the scene. Chapter 7 provides step-by-step instructions on how to excavate buried skeletal remains. Chapter 8 presents a case study that illustrates various methods discussed in the previous chapters, including: the search for a clandestine burial using geophysical technologies, a cadaver dog, and visual methods; excavation techniques; and scene documentation through detailed maps.

We also include two chapters on human and nonhuman skeletal biology at the end of the book. The chapter on human osteology is not designed to teach readers proficiency in human skeletal identification, but rather to assist those readers without a background in osteology in understanding the anatomical terminology used by medical examiners, coroners, forensic odontologists, and forensic anthropologists in their reports. This chapter can also help the reader with creating scene maps in which bones are illustrated. The chapter on nonhuman remains is included to demonstrate that nonhuman bones can easily be mistaken for human bones and to reinforce why an experienced osteologist should make the final determination. This chapter also introduces forensic anthropology students to examples of nonhuman bones that can be easily confused with human bones. These chapters should not be used as a substitute for an expert. All skeletal remains, including those suspected of being nonhuman, should be examined by an expert.

Acknowledgments

The authors would like to extend our thanks to our anonymous reviewers whose comments helped to make this a stronger book. We would also like to thank Crime Scene Investigator Kelly Wood (Orange County Sheriff's Office) and Dr. Michael Spence (University of Western Ontario) for their thoughtful suggestions and editorial comments. Special thanks also to the Orange County Sheriff's Office, Crime Scene Investigator John Mulligan (Orange County Sheriff's Office), and Gene Ralston (Ralston and Associates) for allowing us to use their images.

Authors

Tosha L. Dupras
Department of Sociology and Anthropology, University of Central Florida, Orlando, United States

John J. Schultz
Department of Sociology and Anthropology, University of Central Florida, Orlando, United States

Sandra M. Wheeler
Department of Anthropology, University of Western Ontario, London, Ontario, Canada

Lana J. Williams
Department of Anthropology, University of Western Ontario, London, Ontario, Canada

Author Biographies

Tosha L. Dupras, Ph.D. is an associate professor of anthropology at the University of Central Florida where she teaches human osteology and forensic anthropology. Dr. Dupras received a Master of Science (1995) in human biology from the University of Guelph, and a Ph.D. (1999) in anthropology from McMaster University. She specializes in diet reconstruction through chemical analysis and has been associated with the Dakhleh Oasis Project in Egypt since 1995, where she has excavated in several cemeteries and analyzed many skeletal remains. Dr. Dupras also assists local law enforcement agencies with the search for, excavation of, and analysis of human remains.

John J. Schultz, Ph.D. is an assistant professor of anthropology at the University of Central Florida where he teaches courses in biological anthropology, forensic anthropology, and archaeological sciences. Dr. Schultz received a Master of Science (1998) in human biology from the University of Indianapolis, and a Ph.D. (2003) in anthropology while specializing in forensic anthropology at the University of Florida. His research focuses on taphonomy of human remains, and forensic and archaeological applications of ground-penetrating radar (GPR). Dr. Schultz has conducted extensive GPR research in Florida and has conducted numerous GPR surveys throughout the state for various law enforcement agencies and at cemeteries and archaeological sites.

Sandra M. Wheeler is a doctoral student at the University of Western Ontario where she conducts research in juvenile osteology and paleopathology. She received a graduate certificate in Maya studies (2001) and a Master of Arts in liberal studies (2002) with a focus in anthropology from the University of Central Florida. Wheeler has conducted fieldwork in Belize, Mexico, and Egypt. She has also assisted local law enforcement agencies with the search for and recovery of human remains in Florida and Ontario, Canada.

Lana J. Williams is a doctoral student at the University of Western Ontario where she is conducting research in biochemical methods of mortuary analysis and archaeological sciences. She received a graduate certificate in Maya studies (2001) and a Master of Arts in liberal studies (2002) with a focus in anthropology from the University of Central Florida. Williams has conducted fieldwork in Greece, Belize, and Egypt, and worked as a research assistant with Florida law enforcement in developing new methods for field investigation and reviewing field techniques. She has also assisted local law enforcement agencies with the search for and recovery of human remains in Florida and Ontario, Canada.

Contents

chapter 1

An Introduction to Forensic Anthropology and Forensic Archaeology

During the past two decades, the disciplines of forensic anthropology and forensic archaeology have both received recognition for their potential contributions to crime scene and death investigations. During the 1980s, there was a growing emphasis by forensic anthropologists and archaeologists on the use of proper archaeological field methods when recovering and excavating human remains from forensic contexts (see Berryman and Lahren, 1984; Morse et al., 1983; Sigler-Eisenberg, 1985; Skinner and Lazenby, 1983; Wolf, 1986). The early proponents of forensic archaeology recognized the legal importance of both the utilization of proper collection techniques for human remains and precise documentation of associated contextual information from crime scenes. Although proper archaeological methods are still not practiced universally by forensic anthropologists and crime scene personnel, the continued emphasis in this area throughout the 1990s (Dirkmaat and Adovasio, 1997; France et al., 1992; France et al., 1997; Hunter et al., 1994; Hunter et al., 1996; Killam, 1990; Scott and Connor, 1997) has led to forensic archaeology being recognized as its own discipline.

While both disciplines are highly specialized, and although often thought of as synonymous, there are distinct differences between forensic anthropology and forensic archaeology. In North America, it is common for forensic archaeology to be encompassed within the discipline of forensic anthropology, and in such cases it may be referred to as forensic bioarchaeology (Skinner et al., 2003). However in other locations, such as in the United Kingdom, forensic anthropology and forensic archaeology are considered to be two distinct disciplines. To understand the differences between forensic anthropology and forensic archaeology and the contributions that each can make to crime scene investigation, it is important to start with a discussion of anthropology in general.

Broadly defined, anthropology is the study of humans. The word anthropology derives from the Greek *anthros* (man) and *logos* (the study of).

Anthropologists use a holistic or biocultural approach (a combination of cultural studies and biology) to understand the many facets of human behavior, both past and present. In North America, anthropology is commonly divided into four areas of study, including cultural anthropology, archaeology, linguistics, and physical (biological) anthropology. Cultural anthropology deals with many aspects of human society including but not limited to social structure, behavior, beliefs, and ways of life. Cultural anthropologists mostly work with living societies. Archaeology is the study of past societies, through material remains (such as pottery, stone tools, art, and architecture). Linguistics deals with the evolution of languages and the relationships between languages and societies. In most cases, linguistics is an important aspect of the other areas of anthropology. Physical or biological anthropology deals with the physical and biological aspects of the primate order and includes studies of humans, past and present, and nonhuman primates such as chimpanzees, gorillas, and monkeys. Some of the more specialized areas covered by physical anthropology include:

1. Primatology — the scientific study of nonhuman primates (e.g., apes, monkeys, and prosimians), including their anatomy, behavior, and ecology.
2. Paleoanthropology — the study of ancient hominids through the fossil record in an attempt to reconstruct the evolution and behavior of humans.
3. Human Biology — the study of modern human variation and adaptation.
4. Human growth and development — the study of how humans develop from conception to old age.
5. Nutrition — the study of human nutrition and its effects on human development, both from a modern and evolutionary perspective.
6. Genetics — the study of human DNA from an evolutionary perspective.
7. Osteology — the study of the human skeleton including anatomy, demographics, and pathology.

So where do forensic anthropology and forensic archaeology fit into all of this? By definition, forensic anthropology is the application of physical anthropological theory and methods to answer questions posed in a legal sphere (Iscan, 2001). Anyone interested in becoming a forensic anthropologist must first become a physical anthropologist who specializes in human osteology or human skeletal biology. Osteological analyses can yield clues as to how individuals might have lived, how old they were when they died, whether they were female or male, their state of health (or disease), and the types of trauma they may have experienced related to events such as warfare, occupation, and death. Once the skills of human osteology are mastered, it becomes possible to apply the methods and techniques of analyzing skeletal remains to cases of legal importance. When forensic anthropologists apply methods of skeletal analysis to cases of unidentified modern remains, they are using osteology in a legal context. There are several popular books that document and demonstrate the diverse nature of casework in forensic anthropology and forensic archaeology. These include such examples as Bass' (2003), *Death's Acre*; Browning and Maples' (1995), *Dead Men Do Tell Tales: The Strange and Fascinating Cases of a Forensic Anthropologist*; Ubelaker and Scammell's (2000), *Bones: A Forensic Detective's Casebook*; Rhine's (1998), *Bone Voyage: A Journey in Forensic Anthropology*; and Jackson and Fellenbaum's (2001), *The Bone Detectives: How Forensic Anthropologists Solve Crimes and Uncover Mysteries of the Dead*.

Forensic archaeologists, on the other hand, can arise through different avenues. As a general definition, forensic archaeology is the application of archaeological theory and methods to crime scene excavation and recovery (Hunter, 1996a). Dirkmaat and Adovasio further refine the definition as, "... data collection activities carried out during the field recovery aspect of the entire discipline of forensic anthropology" (1997: 58). In North America, forensic archaeology is another skill set that the forensic anthropologist may attain, thereby combining the two disciplines. In this case, the forensic anthropologist will apply archaeological theory and methods when excavating and documenting crime scenes. In recent years, the number of forensic anthropologists receiving training in archaeological field methods has increased. This increase, in part, is due to many graduate students in forensic anthropology understanding the importance of receiving training in archaeological methods and taking advantage of training in both areas in the same academic department. However, it is possible that the skills of the forensic anthropologist will not include knowledge of archaeological techniques, nor will the forensic archaeologist necessarily have knowledge of human osteology. Therefore, when searching for the appropriate individual to assist in crime scene excavations, local law enforcement agencies should be aware of an individual's skill set before asking for that individual's assistance.

In addition, there are numerous short courses offered around the country that include some type of training in archaeological methods. Although this text is written to assist law enforcement personnel, death investigation personnel, students, and professional forensic anthropologists and archaeologists, training in these methods should be sought. If forensic anthropologists or forensic archaeologists are not available to assist with recoveries, at minimum one, if not all, personnel involved with field collection, search, or recovery should attend a forensic archaeology short course. Information on these courses can be found by doing an Internet search, or through the Web site for the American Academy of Forensic Sciences (http://www.aafs.org/ — select the "meetings" button at the top of the screen).

1.1 What Do Forensic Anthropologists Do?

Traditionally, forensic anthropologists have been requested to assist local law enforcement agencies, medical examiner's offices and coroner's offices, with the identification of human skeletal remains. It is becoming more likely, however, that the forensic anthropologist will be asked to assist in other

Table 1.1 Areas within Human Osteology That the Forensic Anthropologist
Should Have Experience in or Knowledge of for Purposes
of Skeletal Analysis

Biological profile: skeletal indicators of sex, age at death, ancestry, and stature
Unique individual skeletal characteristics or skeletal variation (genetic and
  acquired)
Growth of the human skeleton (familiarity with fetal, infant, and juvenile skeletal
  remains)
Dental development, morphology, and variation
Knowledge of skeletal and dental pathology
Identification of human versus nonhuman skeletal remains
Trauma analysis: distinguishing premortem, perimortem, and postmortem
  modification
Knowledge of taphonomic processes such as decomposition, weathering, and
  animal activity, and how this information can be used to determine time since
  death
Determining context of human skeletal remains: distinguishing archaeological,
  historical, cemetery, anatomical and teaching, and war trophies from forensic
  remains
Experience in analyzing burnt and cremated remains
Knowledge of radiographic analysis of dentition, skeletal material, and objects
Theory and methodology associated with using mitochondrial and nuclear DNA
  for identification
Human soft tissue anatomy
Other identification techniques such as facial reproduction or facial
  superimposition

Source: Modified from Skinner et al., 2003; and Snow, 1982.

capacities. Table 1.1, modified from Skinner and colleagues (2003) and Snow
(1982), includes a list of skills that the forensic anthropologist should be
experienced in or knowledgeable about.

In addition to the skills listed in Table 1.1, the forensic anthropologist,
regardless of archaeological knowledge, may also be able to assist in searching
crime scenes and recovering skeletal remains. Because forensic anthropologists
are trained in recognizing human skeletal remains, they may be able to provide
valuable assistance in locating missing skeletal elements. This was true in the
case shown in Figure 1.1. Authors Dupras and Williams assisted in analyzing
human skeletal remains that were excavated without the assistance of a forensic
anthropologist. After removing the recovered remains from clothing and a
mass of roots, initial skeletal analysis and examination of the scene photos
revealed that several bones that should have been present were missing. Upon
revisiting the site, several more bones were recovered (Figure 1.1). To the
layperson it may seem that missing a few bones would be inconsequential,
but these bones could be the ones that hold the key to individual identification,
and also aid in reconstructing what happened to the individual. In addition,
it may also save time, money, and resources in the future by avoiding a

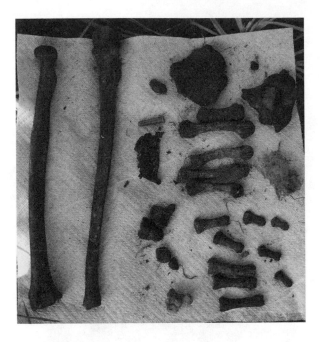

Figure 1.1 Missing bones and evidence that were later discovered when a forensic anthropologist revisited the scene.

situation in which someone might discover the missing bones well after the case is closed, therefore creating what appears to be a new case.

Of particular importance is the fact that forensic anthropologists are also trained in recognizing patterns of taphonomy (what happens to a body after the individual dies), and they may be able to help locate remains based on these processes. Forensic anthropologists can also readily identify fetal, infant, and child skeletal remains, which often look very different from adult human skeletal remains and can be easily overlooked by the untrained eye. Also, as explained previously, many forensic anthropologists are knowledgeable in archaeological methods and are trained in meticulous excavation techniques. As with searches, knowledge of the human skeleton can be beneficial at this stage of recovery.

1.2 What Do Forensic Archaeologists Do?

As a separate discipline, or as a set of skills that the forensic anthropologist may possess, forensic archaeology involves applying archaeological techniques to the crime scene. It is important to recognize that there are fundamental differences between traditional academic archaeology and forensic archaeology (Hunter, 2002). Traditional academic archaeology is research based and question driven, where particular methodological steps are consistently followed. The forensic archaeologist, on the other hand, in addition to applying methodological steps, has to deal with law enforcement and legal procedures, major time constraints, the media, occasionally the presence of

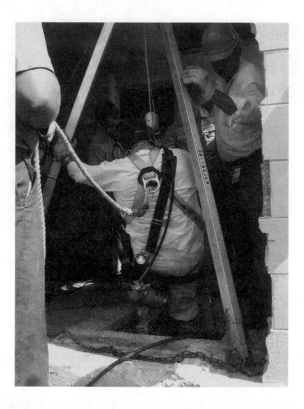

Figure 1.2 Lowering a well-protected city worker into a sewage-holding tank in search of human remains.

soft tissue, and situations in which traditional steps in archaeological methods will not work. Forensic archaeologists have to be much more flexible in their approach, and adapt their methods to each crime scene (Hoshower, 1998). As an example, two of the authors, Dupras and Schultz, were engaged in a case that involved searching for a missing person whose remains might have been deposited in a city sewage-holding tank. Due to the potential lethal hazards associated with this site, all the material had to first be removed from the holding tank. This was accomplished by lowering heavily protected individuals into the tank, outfitted with oxygen so they would not succumb to deadly gases (Figure 1.2). These individuals used a large vacuum to suction the material into a waiting tanker truck. The material was then deposited on the ground and sieved through large screens in an attempt to recover any remains (Figure 1.3). In this case, there was no possible way to apply traditional archaeological techniques throughout the recovery process.

Forensic archaeologists should possess or have knowledge of all the skills associated with traditional archaeology, in addition to understanding how to apply these skills in a forensic context. A list of these skills, drawn from the authors' experience and modified from Skinner et al. (2003) can be found in Table 1.2.

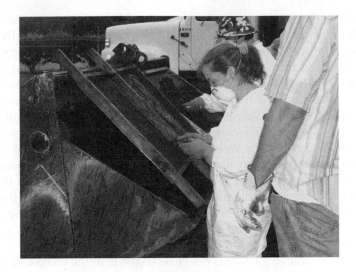

Figure 1.3   Author Tosha Dupras (center), Orange County crime scene investigator Kelly Wood (back), and Orange County homicide detective Dave Clarke (right) sieving through materials removed from the sewage-holding tank.

It is becoming more evident that there are two important roles that are directly associated with the forensic archaeologist (Skinner et al., 2003; Spennemann and Franke, 1995). The first role of the forensic archaeologist includes the skills and techniques needed in order to understand and interpret the prolonged history of crime scene transformation, in other words, the taphonomic events that occur after a site has been created. The results of taphonomic

Table 1.2 Skills or Knowledge Associated with Forensic Archaeology

Ground search methods (e.g., environmental changes associated with burials)
Survey techniques (e.g., compass, theodolite, total station)
Geophysical search methods (e.g., GPR, electromagnetic survey, metal detector)
Site formation analysis and description
Mapping techniques
Spatial controls (e.g., establishing datum points, GPS, establishing grids)
Uses of heavy equipment (when use is appropriate and how excavations should
  be performed)
Excavation techniques (including screening)
Basic recognition of human and nonhuman skeletal anatomy
Artifact collection, documentation and preservation
Site recording (e.g., casting of features, digital and still photography,
  documentation)
Field sample collection (e.g., soil, botanical, entomological)
Collection and preservation of skeletal remains and associated evidence

Source: Modified from Skinner et al., 2003.

events will be the first thing that is encountered by the team of investigators, and the interpretation of these transformations can be vital during the search and recovery process. For example, the intensity of taphonomic processes was realized firsthand by Dupras during her involvement in a skeletal recovery near Niagara Falls. In this case, the individual was discovered on a steep slope at the base of a cliff face. It was soon recognized that this site was annually exposed to excessive water runoff from melting snow, continual falling rock from the cliff face, and landscape alteration from a combination of water and falling rock. As a result, the skeleton was dispersed from the top of the slope to the bottom, with the cranial and upper body elements being located near the top, and the lower body being deposited toward the bottom of the slope. As the body decomposed, different parts moved down the slope as the terrain changed each year due to taphonomic processes. An understanding of these geologic and taphonomic processes aided in developing the search and excavation techniques employed to recover this individual.

The second role of the forensic archaeologist is in the reconstruction and interpretation of the events that occurred as the scene was being created and the body deposited. Meticulous archaeological techniques can assist in recreating the scene, and can also be used to corroborate or disprove assailant stories about what happened at a particular scene. An example of such a case occurred when the authors, Dupras, Wheeler, and Williams, became involved in a case in which the assailant had already been convicted of murder and given the death penalty without the body being discovered. As the assailant's time on death row was coming to an end, an agreement was made with the prosecutor stipulating that the assailant was required to

Figure 1.4   Authors Lana Williams (left) and Sandra Wheeler (right) documenting a scene in which large pieces of metal had been placed over the body. The discovery of the metal strips matched the story given by the incarcerated assailant.

provide all the details of the murder and reveal the location of the body. The assailant gave specific details of the crime, location, and orientation of the body, including the process by which he created the grave. One specific detail that was provided described the body being covered with large pieces of metal. Because the agreement was dependent on the truthfulness of the assailant's story, it was imperative that meticulous excavation techniques be used and all details be recorded in order to recreate the events that occurred during the deposition of the body. Figure 1.4 shows authors Williams and Wheeler documenting the discovery of the large metal strips that covered the body (for more detail see Chapter 8).

1.3 Where Are Forensic Anthropologists and Forensic Archaeologists Employed?

In most instances, forensic anthropologists do not have full-time positions in which they actively work on forensic cases. The majority of forensic anthropologists and forensic archaeologists in North America are employed as professors at universities or other academic institutes. In these instances, when their field or lab skills are needed, practicing forensic anthropologists are consulted by law enforcement agencies, medical examiners, and coroners. In rare instances, forensic anthropologists and forensic archaeologists may be employed by museums. For example, when the FBI needs the expertise of a forensic anthropologist, it turns to the Smithsonian Institution (http://www.si.edu), which has a number of physical and biological anthropologists who specialize in forensic anthropology (Ubelaker and Scamell, 2000). In addition, forensic anthropologists are employed in jobs outside of academics. For example, medical examiner's or coroner's offices occasionally hire forensic anthropologists for another role in the office, and they may work on forensic anthropology casework when the need arises. Forensic anthropologists may also be hired full time by medical examiner's offices if they are located in regions that can support a full-time caseload.

The single largest employer of forensic anthropologists and forensic archaeologists in the United States is the Joint POW/MIA Accounting Command ([JPAC] http://www.jpac.pacom.mil), located on the island of Oahu in Hawaii. JPAC was formed in October 2003 with the joining of the U.S. Army Central Identification Laboratory Hawaii (formerly called CILHI), and the Joint Task Force – Full Accounting. One of the missions of JPAC is to account for all Americans missing as a consequence of any conflicts involving the United States. As a result, teams of forensic anthropologists and forensic archaeologists perform searches and recoveries in countries where there are reports of remains belonging to American citizens.

Forensic anthropologists and forensic archaeologists are also recognized for their expertise in the identification of individuals involved in mass disasters such as plane crashes (for example, TWA Flight 800), earthquakes, floods, or bombings (such as the Oklahoma City Federal Building and the World Trade Center in New York City). In the United States, most state and federal mass disaster teams, known as the Disaster Mortuary Operational Response Teams (DMORT, http://www.dmort.org), have several forensic anthropologists and forensic archaeologists on their rosters. In addition, other government agencies that employ forensic anthropologists in a full-time capacity include the National Transportation and Safety Board (NTSB, http://www.ntsb.gov) and the Armed Forces Institute of Pathology (AFIP, http://www.afip.org).

Since the 1980s, forensic anthropologists and forensic archaeologists have become vital team members in the search, recovery, and identification of victims of human rights violations around the world. Agencies such as Physicians for Human Rights and the United Nations International Criminal Tribunals routinely employ forensic anthropologists and forensic archaeologists in locations such as Guatemala, Argentina, Bosnia, Rwanda, and East Timor to assist in the identification of individuals who have died as a result of their ethnicity, political affiliation, or religious beliefs.

1.4   How to Find a Forensic Anthropologist or Forensic Archaeologist

1.4.1   American Academy of Forensic Sciences

The American Academy of Forensic Sciences (AAFS) is a nonprofit organization comprised of forensic specialists in the following sections: criminalistics, engineering sciences, general, jurisprudence, odontology, pathology and biology, physical anthropology, psychiatry and behavioral sciences, questioned documents, and toxicology. The AAFS has members from all 50 of the United States, Canada, and 50 other countries worldwide. To achieve recognition within the broader discipline of forensic sciences in North America, most forensic anthropologists belong to the Physical Anthropology section of the AAFS. There are certain qualifications that must be met to become a member of the Academy. For the Physical Anthropology section, members must demonstrate through casework, teaching, or research that they are active in the discipline. Please note however, that this does not mean that the individual has been certified as an expert in forensic anthropology.

One option for locating members of the discipline is to visit the Web site for the American Academy of Forensic Sciences. Unfortunately, access to the membership directory is now restricted to Academy members. If you or your agency has a membership, you can find a list of Academy members in your area by following these instructions:

- Log on to the official Web site for the Academy of Forensic Sciences, which can be found at http://www.aafs.org.
- Select "Membership" at the top of the page, and then select "find a member" from the pull-down menu.
- Enter desired "State" and leave "Last Name" and "City" blank.
- Under "Section" choose "Anth."

This should result in a list of forensic anthropologists with contact information.

1.4.2 American Board of Forensic Anthropology

A growing number of members of the Physical Anthropology section of the AAFS have received certification or Diplomat status from the American Board of Forensic Anthropology. Diplomat status is the highest recognized form of certification in the discipline of forensic anthropology in North America. To obtain this certification, individuals must have a doctoral degree in anthropology with an emphasis in physical anthropology, have three years of professional experience, and must pass a comprehensive written and practical examination. Currently, there are approximately 69 members listed as board certified, while perhaps only about 60 of these are practicing forensic anthropologists. For a list and contact information for forensic anthropologists with Diplomat status, visit the American Board of Forensic Anthropology (ABFA) Web site (http://www.csuchico.edu/anth/ABFA/).

Unfortunately, at this time, there are no recognized associations or boards specifically for forensic archaeology, and because of this, there are no easy ways to find individuals who have skills in forensic archaeology. The best way to find these specialists, particularly in North America, is to contact individuals who identify themselves as forensic anthropologists and inquire as to their skills in the realm of forensic archaeology. Another option, if forensic specialists are not available in your area, is to contact local universities that have field archaeologists on staff. Even though these individuals may not be trained in the forensic context, they will still possess all the necessary archaeological skills to conduct excavations.

chapter 2

Tools and Equipment

The forensic archaeologist should be well prepared and have all the tools and equipment necessary to perform searches and excavations, and should not rely on local law enforcement to provide the necessary tools. Since the search and recovery of human remains is not a common type of crime scene for most law enforcement agencies, it is not surprising that most agencies will not have this specialized equipment. The variety of tools and equipment used by forensic archaeologists during excavation is practically limitless but the following chapter provides descriptions of the basic, most helpful tools commonly used in the forensic recovery of human remains. Figure 2.1 shows an example of a field excavation kit containing the necessary tools. More specialized search equipment is discussed in Chapter 4, and associated equipment needed for the procurement of entomological and botanical evidence is discussed in Chapter 5. Although some of the tools and equipment are purchased through specialty stores (see Table 2.1), the majority are available at local home hardware stores. A checklist of basic field equipment can be found in Appendix 1.

2.1 Search and Site Preparation Equipment

When beginning a search, each individual should be equipped with a bundle of brightly colored survey flags that can be used to mark the locations of scattered evidence. In addition, survey flags and survey tape can be used to mark the entrance and exit locations to the site. Small hand machetes and handsaws are helpful in clearing plant growth from the surrounding work areas and around any associated evidence (Figure 2.2). Investigators should be especially vigilant when clearing underbrush or leaf cover, since evidence can easily become lodged at the base of trees or in other plant materials. Hand loppers (Figure 2.2) are useful for cutting thick underbrush or branches, wire or cables, and any other heavy materials that impede investigation or obstruct the work area.

When specifically searching for buried bodies or evidence, a variety of probes can be used and should be included as standard field equipment.

Figure 2.1   Equipment and cases shown in the field.

The most common probes used are the basic T-bar probe and a soil-coring probe, used to detect soil disturbances. A detailed description of the different kinds of probes, and their proper uses can be found in Chapter 6.

2.2   Field Excavation Equipment

When removing surface debris such as leaf litter and vegetation, a plastic fan-shaped rake (Figure 2.3) should be used. Spade and flat shovels are useful when removing large quantities of soil, but they should never be used as excavation tools once the burial site has been located. Spade shovels should only be used to backfill holes or move soil that has already been screened from one location to another if necessary. Flat shovels (Figure 2.3) are typically used to remove very thin layers of soil from surface areas or to cut and remove sod from yards or fields.

Hand trowels (Figure 2.4) are used for precise excavation, especially when removing soil surrounding bones or objects where larger tools would damage or displace evidence. With a bit of practice, a pointed hand trowel with a straight blade can be used for extremely delicate work and may prove to be the most effective tool in the field kit. Four- or five-in cement trowels made of drop-forged steel are recommended as the handles, blade welds, and points are more resistant to breakage. Square-edged trowels are perfect for excavating in sandy or wet soils (Figure 2.4). Some of the more popular brands used by archaeologists include Marshalltown or Goldblatt. Cheap trowels will bend or break and can put an end to any excavation quickly if the site is miles from the nearest hardware store. Garden-variety trowels with curved blades are not suited for excavation and should not be used in any recovery of human remains. In addition, garden claw tools should never be used for excavating. Trowel edges should be sharpened with a rat-tail file to aid in removing heavier

Table 2.1 Contact Information for Companies That Sell Equipment Used for Forensic Archaeology

Company	Contact Information	Examples of Equipment Available
Forestry Suppliers, Inc.	205 West Franklin Street Jackson, MS 39201 Phone: 1-800-647-5368 Fax: 1-800-543-4203 http://www. forestry-suppliers.com/	Chaining stakes Metric measuring tapes Compasses GPS String Probes Trowels
Ben Meadows Company	P.O. Box 5277 Janesville, WI 53547-5277 Phone: 1-800-241-6401 Fax: 1-800-628-2068 http://www. benmeadows.com/	Basic surveying equipment Flags Flagging tape Compasses
Evident Crime Scene Products	739 Brooks Mill Road Union Hall, VA 24176 Phone: 1-800-576-7606 Fax: 1-888-384-3368 http://www.evident crimescene.com/	Photographic scales North arrows Evidence markers Crime scene tape Entomology kits
Lynn Peavey Company	10749 W. 84th Terrace P.O. Box 14100 Lenexa, KS 66285-4100 Phone: 1-800-255-6499 Fax: 1-913-495-6787 http://www. lynnpeavey.com/	Entomology kits Evidence packages Casting materials
Arrowhead Forensic Products	14400 College Blvd. Suite 100 Lenexa, KS 66215 Phone: 1-913-894-8388 Fax: 1-913-894-8399 http://www. crime-scene.com/	Evidence packages Casting materials Photo scales Evidence markers Evidence packages
Lightening Powder Company, Inc.	13386 International Parkway Jacksonville, FL 32218 Phone: 1-800-852-0300 Fax: 1-800-588-0399 http://www.redwop.com	Casting materials Photographic scales Evidence markers

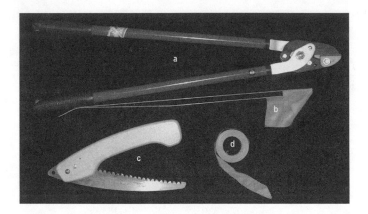

Figure 2.2   Equipment used during survey and clearing: (a) hand loppers; (b) survey flags; (c) hand saw; and (d) survey tape.

soils and cutting small roots when excavating. Always clean and wipe down trowels with light oil after each use to prevent rust.

Wood sculpting tools, splints, bamboo skewers, or spoons (each kit should have a variety of sizes of spoons, and plastic is preferred) are ideal for detailing

Figure 2.3   Equipment used for site clearing and excavation: (a) fan rake; (b) flat-edged shovel; (c) collapsible sawhorse; and (d) screen.

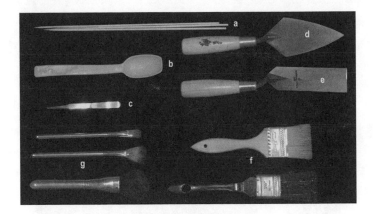

Figure 2.4   Equipment used during excavation: (a) bamboo skewers; (b) plastic spoon; (c) tweezers; (d) pointed trowel; (e) square trowel; (f) paint brushes; and (g) makeup brushes.

around bone surfaces without scratching or nicking the bone (Figure 2.4). Dental picks may also be used, but only with extreme care to avoid producing any misleading or erroneous marks on the bone surfaces. Small tweezers are useful for removing small items or for evidence collection. In some cases, it may be preferable to use disposable skewers or plastic items when detailing around remains in extremely wet conditions or if any soft tissue is still present.

Soft horsehair, China bristle, or other natural bristle brushes, such as paint or make-up, are recommended in excavation to brush away loose soil from the remains before photographing or drawing (Figure 2.4). Natural brushes tend to last longer than synthetic bristle brushes and have less of a tendency to clump in sandy or wet clay soils. These brushes are less likely to lose bristles. A variety of sizes of paint brushes should be included in each kit. Make-up brushes are a smaller, softer alternative for very delicate excavation. It is recommended that all brushes be cleaned with a 2% bleach-to-water solution after each excavation to avoid any possibility of contamination and transfer of materials to the next recovery scene.

Root clippers are needed for trimming roots and small ground cover (Figure 2.5). Never pull any roots or plant material since this can easily dislodge or destroy evidence. Always trim roots away from the exposed burial walls and floor while excavating. This will help make other items in drawings and photographs appear more clearly. Wisk brooms are useful in removing loose dirt from surrounding areas but should never be used directly on the remains as they may become displaced or damaged (Figure 2.5). Heavy plastic or metal dustpans can be used along with whisk brooms when collecting loose soil from larger cleared spaces within the excavation or in the surrounding area (Figure 2.5). Avoid the use of flimsy metal or plastic dustpans that will bend or break when they are used with heavy soil. Sturdy plastic or metal buckets (spackle buckets work best) are used to transport soil for screening (Figure 2.5).

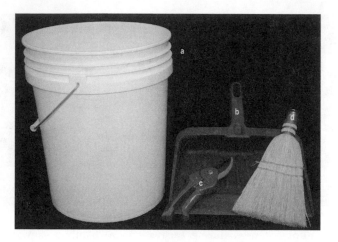

Figure 2.5   Equipment used for clearing and excavation: (a) spackle bucket; (b) plastic dustpan; (c) root clippers; and (d) whisk broom.

Screens with 1/4-in mesh are typically used for sifting through soil that has been removed from the excavation to recover materials that may otherwise be overlooked (Figure 2.3). A smaller gauge screen mesh may be attached to an 8 in ×10 in wooden picture frame for screening very small elements, such as fetal bones or insect casings, that would normally be missed using the larger gauge screens. Mesh can be either metal or plastic, and both should be thoroughly cleaned after each use. Collapsible sawhorses (Figure 2.3) are an excellent platform for screening materials. By laying the screen across the sawhorses, there is a clear view of the materials and a relatively flat, level working surface. Plastic sheeting or tarps should be placed beneath the screens to catch the screened soil. This method also allows for the screened material to be kept separate. In case finer screening is necessary, simply change out the plastic sheeting or tarps from under the work area. After each bucket of soil is completely screened, the tarp or sheeting can be used to take the soil to the collection pile. Tarps and plastic sheeting can also be used to cover an excavation in case of rain or to protect the excavation overnight.

2.3 Mapping and Measuring Equipment

A transit is used with a stadia rod for measuring precise angles and distances from fixed points. These points are used to plot the survey map, plan, and section drawings of the site. A total station can also be used for this purpose, however, it is an expensive piece of equipment and requires a trained operator. A hand compass is useful in the site survey and also in determining the orientation of burials relative to other features, such as posts, trees, or buildings.

Metric measuring tapes are indispensable tools during the mapping and excavation processes, and the more and different kinds that are available,

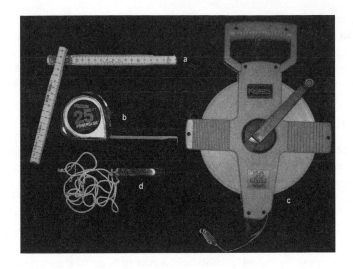

Figure 2.6   Equipment used for measurement: (a) folding stick tape; (b) hand measuring tape; (c) 50-m tape; and (d) plumb bob.

the better. A 30- to 50-m hand tape (Figure 2.6) that can be clipped to the belt is a must. At least two 30-m to 50-m field tapes should also be included in the toolkit, as these are needed for mapping any areas of recovery (Figure 2.6). Metric folding stick tapes are also handy for drawing and taking depth measurements. Plumb bobs with a 2- to 5-oz weight and string line levels are crucial for plotting the exact location of evidence and for measuring depths (Figure 2.6).

Survey string is a strong, nonstretch string that is typically white, florescent pink, or yellow (Figure 2.7). We recommend bright colors that can be seen easily.

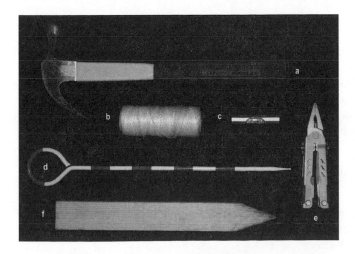

Figure 2.7   Equipment used for constructing grids: (a) metal hammer; (b) survey string; (c) line level; (d) chaining stake; (e) multipurpose tool; and (f) wooden stake.

It can be used to define area limits, grid an excavation, or can be used with the plumb bob and line level. Heavy, large nails, wooden, or survey chaining stakes, and flagging tape can all be used in laying out an excavation grid and marking survey instrument locations or datum points. A small metal hammer or rubber mallet can be used to drive the stakes into the ground (Figure 2.7).

2.4   Drawing and Recording Equipment

Photographic scales and a north arrow (a pointed trowel can substitute for a north arrow) should be used in all photography to note scale and orientation of any evidence. All necessary blank forms, paper evidence bags, labels, tags, notebooks, pens, permanent markers, and pencils should be on hand to properly record and collect materials. Tools needed for a detailed drawing of the excavation would include: several mechanical pencils with extra leads and erasers, nails or chaining stakes, survey string, compass, handheld measuring tapes, folding stick tapes, line level, plumb bob, a pad of 5- or 10-squares-per-centimeter graph paper, and a drawing board, clipboard, or field desk. A waterproof field notebook can also be very useful in bad weather conditions.

2.5   Optional Equipment

With field conditions varying from scene to scene, it is always best to keep a few optional items available in case any adverse conditions or special circumstances arise. A first aid kit is a necessity in the field. Any cuts or scrapes acquired during excavation should be attended to as soon as possible to prevent severe infections. Breathing masks are helpful in extremely dusty or odorous conditions as well as cases with heavy infestations of insects.

Additional items that may be useful include:

- Multipurpose tool or Swiss Army knife for any minor tool needs that may occur.
- Hand lens or magnifying glass for close inspection of remains or associated evidence.
- Water spray bottles can be used to keep the sides of an excavation from collapsing in sandy or dry soils.
- Soil color charts for accurate color identification of the soils associated with the remains.

Other useful items that can make your work environment much more tolerable when spending time doing detailed tasks:

- Fresh drinking water
- Snacks
- Bug spray
- Sunscreen
- Flashlights
- Hats

- Extra batteries for all equipment
- Latex gloves and canvas- or leather-work gloves
- Foam knee pads or mat
- Hand sanitizer
- Disposable coveralls
- Extra clothing
- Extra pair of shoes and socks

chapter 3

Search Techniques Used in Locating Human Remains

In forensic investigation, searches are performed to locate clandestine burials, bodies deposited on the surface, body parts, skeletal elements or bones, and associated evidence. At the same time, searches can also be utilized in clearing areas so investigations can continue in additional suspected areas. Before conducting a search, a search plan should be formulated that identifies the personnel and equipment that will be needed and the specific search techniques that will be used.

Most searches will have a greater rate of success employing multiple methods (France et al., 1992; France et al., 1997). Search techniques can be either nonintrusive or intrusive. Nonintrusive searches use nondestructive methods in which searches are performed by visually looking for evidence of a burial or surface scatter on the ground. Nonintrusive searches also include cadaver dogs and almost all of the geophysical prospecting methods that can be used in areas with relatively no obstructions or in areas that are fairly restricted in size. Conversely, intrusive searches use destructive methods that can damage bodies and evidence. Intrusive methods are used when nonintrusive methods are not successful, and as a follow-up to visual search methods. Intrusive searches include probing and coring the soil, digging test excavations, and using heavy equipment.

One benefit of having a forensic anthropologist on-site during the search phase is the identification of potentially significant physical evidence *in situ*. Most forensic anthropologists can give a quick evaluation of remains to determine the following:

- Nonhuman vs. human remains
- Forensic vs. nonforensic skeletal remains (e.g., historic and prehistoric)
- Missing skeletal elements that may still be within the search area

3.1   Types of Search Areas

There are three basic types of areas that can be separately defined when searching for human remains: open, obstructed, and submerged areas (Killam, 1990). Open areas can be searched using aerial reconnaissance, walking grids, or remote sensing techniques. These areas include fields, flatlands, backyards, or any area that is primarily open to a 360° field of vision. Searchers tend to have the most success in locating remains in open areas. Urban development, wooded areas, caves, and any other landscape feature that impedes search techniques are defined as obstructed areas in which it becomes more difficult to locate remains, especially if the remains are buried in areas where visual obstructions occur. Underwater searches require specialized equipment and personnel. The search and mapping techniques used in submerged areas are specific to each individual case and are less commonly utilized.

3.2   Planning the Search

The preparation is just as important as the search itself. Prior to beginning every search, carefully determine the boundaries of the area to be searched and the different methods that will be used. If a large area is to be searched, geographic or topographic maps and aerial photographs can be helpful in providing specific information about the terrain and area to be searched (see section 6.7 in Chapter 6 for map resources). Maps and aerial photographs can be useful in determining how to divide the area for searching, as well as determining which search methods will be used. Maps and photographs can also be used to show any changes in the terrain that may have occurred since the body was buried. For example, an aerial photograph of the area at the time the body was thought to have been buried and a photograph from the present day should be compared to determine how the landscape has changed and whether the body is in an area that is still accessible. If a structure, road, or pavement was placed over the body after it was buried, traditional search methods will not work. In addition, the planning phase should also include a preliminary reconnaissance of the search area to learn more about the terrain, the different search methods that can be used, and any specialized equipment that will be needed.

The planning phase should also entail learning as much as possible about the body deposition or burial process. For example, if a search is planned to locate a buried homicide victim, detectives and investigators need to learn as much about the burial process as possible when talking to informants and assailants. Specific information learned about the burial process may dictate which search methods will be appropriate. See Table 3.1 for specific questions to ask about forensic bodies that have been buried to conceal their location. Finally, on the day of the search, make sure there are enough personnel to carry out the surface search in the designated area, that all the equipment and experts are arriving when expected, and that refreshments are provided for the searchers.

Table 3.1 Questions for Investigators to Ask Suspects or Informants about a Burial Prior to a Search

When did the event occur?

How deep was the body buried?

Was the body wrapped in anything and was the body clothed when it was buried?

Was anything placed over the body (such as boards, concrete, metal debris, or even a pet or a second individual) before the grave was filled?

What were the local conditions of the area (e.g., dry or moist ground, open or wooded area)?

Was anything placed over the grave (such as brush, trash, tree limbs) to conceal its location?

Were there any unique landmarks near the burial that may be helpful to locate the burial during the search?

Has the landscape changed since the body was buried?

3.2.1   Visual Foot Searches

Visual foot searches involve nonintrusive techniques commonly used in archaeology and forensic investigations in which archaeological sites or forensic evidence are located by means of eyesight. When searching large areas or areas with obstructions, the total search area should be divided into smaller zones that are easily managed in a day or less. Therefore, the total search area can be divided into smaller manageable search areas that follow existing boundaries formed by natural and cultural (human-made) obstructions or features. For example, natural obstructions can include streams, other bodies of water, hills, and cliffs, and cultural obstructions can include buildings, fences, roads, and parking lots. After boundaries of the search area have been determined for a visual search, a pattern must be chosen for an effective and thorough search of the defined area. The pattern should maximize available staff resources for the most efficient results. Three of the most effective patterns for searching the surface of an area are a strip pattern, a grid pattern, and a circular pattern.

3.2.1.1   Strip or Line Search

The most frequently used pattern for searches is called a line search and it will provide 100% coverage if performed properly (Figure 3.1a). Searchers line up in a straight line and are positioned close enough to one another so that their field of view overlaps (Figure 3.2). Depending on the size of the search team and the area to be searched, the individuals will search an area by walking first in one direction and then in the opposite direction. After the team completes one line of the search area, it will complete an adjacent line in the opposite direction. The boundary of the area that is searched can be marked by the farthest person on the line with flagging tape. Each search line should be directed by a team leader who can follow behind the line, or be positioned in the middle of the search line, to maintain the pace of the search. Also, if the search team is looking for

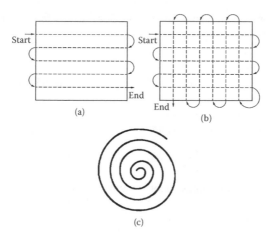

Figure 3.1   Search patterns: (a) line or strip search; (b) grid search; and (c) spiral search.

human bones or a complete skeleton, a forensic anthropologist can follow behind the line and inspect any item that a searcher thinks may be human bone or related to a burial.

The line should only move at a pace that is slow enough to allow all of the searchers ample time to view the ground in their lanes. It is the job of the team leader to make sure that searchers do not get too far ahead of the group. Whenever individuals in the line get too far ahead, the leader should direct the pace of the line to get team members back in a straight line, or stop the line to allow those working at a slower pace to catch up. Whenever the line has stopped, only the leader can direct the line to start again. Team members should carry pin flags and mark any evidence or anything potentially significant

Figure 3.2   Searchers performing a line or strip search.

in their respective lanes. When one team member locates potential evidence he or she should call out to the entire line to stop and everyone in the line should do a detailed search of the immediate area. After everyone has finished their detailed search, then the team leader can direct the search line to continue moving again.

3.2.1.2   Grid Search

A more time-consuming variation of the line search is called a grid search (Figure 3.1b). Once the line search pattern is completed, the search team will search the same area in a perpendicular direction. This pattern provides 200% coverage because the ground is searched twice. The main advantage of this method is that the ground is searched from two directions and multiple angles. Using this pattern increases the potential for discovering skeletal material or evidence that it was not possible to see from another angle.

3.2.1.3   Circular Pattern

A circular pattern works best when the search team and search area are small, or if the search starts on the top of a hill (Figure 3.1c). Killam (1990) suggests using the spiral pattern as a one-person search method in which the searcher moves in decreasing concentric circles (outside toward the inside) within a small search area. This method should usually be used from outside to inside so evidence is not inadvertently trampled during the initial search. However, there are instances when it is more appropriate to reverse this pattern starting the search initially inside and moving in a circular pattern toward the outside. This interior-to-exterior pattern is often used when searching for missing bones that may have been dragged away by carnivores from a known primary deposition site. The circular pattern would begin at the location of the primary deposition site and continue outward in increasing concentric circles as more bones are located.

3.3   *Other Recommendations for Visual Searches*

The degree of difficulty in conducting a visual search is directly related to the landscape features. An open field provides ideal landscape conditions for searching. However, as the number of obstructions increase in the search area, it becomes more difficult to locate evidence and bones. In search areas with scrub brush or other forms of ground cover, team members should be placed closer together to allow for more detailed searching in and around undergrowth. The leader should also slow the pace of the search in areas of dense undergrowth to increase the amount of time the team is searching. It is important to remember that crime scenes can be three-dimensional. Evidence and bones can be found in other locations in addition to being deposited on the ground. In forested areas, it is sometimes helpful to look up since remains can be deposited in tree limbs by various means. For example, when searching a scene involving a plane crash in a wooded area, it is recommended that a visual search of the forest canopy is included to locate items deposited in the trees.

3.4   Briefing Team Members Prior to a Search

After the search plan is devised, all team members must be briefed on the rules and procedures for the search. It should not be assumed that all team members have prior experience in conducting visual searches. When large searches are conducted, there could be numerous volunteers that have no experience search- ing for graves and bones, and as a result they would not know what indicators to look for that would signify a possible grave. Prior to starting the surface search, all search team members should be briefed on the following:

- Areas to be covered
- Patterns to use for the search
- Specific directions for the visual search
- Possible visual indicators
- Time constraints

3.5   Indicators to Look for When Searching for Burials and Surface Remains

3.5.1   Locating Surface Scatters

There are numerous indicators to look for that may be helpful when searching for a skeleton or burial. A skeleton deposited on the ground surface will obvi- ously be easier to locate than a body that was buried in order to hide its location. Surface deposits will be identified by visually locating bones and soft tissue, clothing and personal possessions, and other forms of evidence that are asso- ciated with the remains such as material used to wrap a body (for example, rugs, tarps, plastic sheeting, plastic bags). It is also important to search through trash and brush that may be placed over a body to conceal its whereabouts, and determine whether there is any evidence of animal activity and scavenging.

Recent surface deposits can also be located via decomposition scent using cadaver dogs (see section 3.6 in this chapter). However, surface deposits that have been on the surface for multiple years can be difficult to recognize. Table 3.2 provides a summary of indicators that are used to locate surface deposits. Over time, the bones, clothing and other evidence can deteriorate from weathering and plant growth and become difficult to recognize on the ground. For example, weathered bones can turn white in

Table 3.2 A Summary of Indicators Used to Locate Surface Depositions

Skeletal remains and soft tissue
Clothing, personal objects, and weapons
Decomposition odor
Loose trash or brush heaps
Animal activity and scavenging
Materials used for wrapping body

color from sun bleaching, or dark in color from soil staining. In addition, bones can become more difficult to locate as they become covered by fallen leaf litter or partially buried by long-term exposure to soil erosion from rainfall or natural settling.

3.5.2 Locating Disarticulated and Dispersed Remains

Remains deposited in outdoor environments usually exhibit some degree of dispersal of skeletal elements. Some common causes of skeletal dispersal include taphonomic processes such as animal activity, gravity, human activity, and fluvial (water) transport, as well as soil formation processes such as mechanical alterations to sediments due to burrowing animals, plant roots, tree-falls, freeze-thaw mixing, and slumping of the soil layers. Therefore, proper search strategies are important in delineating site boundaries, locating scattered skeletal elements, locating the primary depositional site of the remains, and determining the original position of the body.

Upon detection of scattered surface remains, it is important not only to search the areas of highest concentration of skeletal elements, but also to continue searching further in outlying zones where fewer scattered elements may exist. Natural features that may direct dispersal patterns should be considered when searching for missing elements. For example, if a body was deposited on an incline, gravity, wind, and rain could move missing elements further down the hill to a lower level. In this example, the search for missing elements should include searching downhill from the primary deposition site.

In many instances, dispersal of skeletal remains results from carnivore activity spreading skeletal elements over a large area. Visual searches should be conducted to locate missing skeletal remains that may be found in thick brush and within animal burrows where animals tend to deposit bones that were scavenged from the primary depositional site. Furthermore, it may be possible to infer the direction that missing elements were dragged away from the primary deposit site after the site has been properly cleaned of debris and documented. For instance, after cleaning a site of debris and mapping the location of skeletal elements, it is noted that there are missing elements and that scavenged bones have been dragged in one direction from the primary deposit. In this case, it may be possible to easily locate missing skeletal elements in a wooded environment with thick underbrush by inferring directionality from the orientation of the primary deposit to the scavenged remains. The search for additional bones can begin by first starting in the direction of the scavenged bones, and spreading out from there if the remains are not located.

The most difficult skeletal elements to locate in the field are the teeth because of their small size. When the body decomposes, the anterior teeth (incisors and canines) separate early from the jaws during the decomposition process and will separate much more easily from their sockets than molars because they have single roots (as opposed to molars which have two or more roots). It is important to locate as many teeth as possible for identification purposes and it may be possible to locate them with appropriate search strategies. Haglund (1997b) outlines search strategies used in locating missing teeth associated with remains scattered by medium-sized canids. It is recommended that not only the primary deposition site be searched for teeth, but also secondary deposition sites and along the directional paths that skeletal elements may have traveled. Haglund (1997c) also brings attention to special circumstances that might bias predictable patterns of canid scattering, such as preexisting facial trauma, terrain, or purposeful dismemberment by humans. In these circumstances, it may not be possible to predict the correct location of missing teeth.

3.5.2.1 Common Taphonomic Processes That Disarticulate and Disperse Skeletal Remains

When the term taphonomy is used in forensic archaeology, it is in reference to the postmortem time period and the changes or modifications that occur to bodies and skeletal remains after death. Taphonomic analysis begins at the scene with the reconstruction of the postdepositional history of the body or skeleton in question. One of the more common postdepositional processes that must be reconstructed is disarticulation and dispersal of decomposing bodies. There is usually some degree of dispersal of skeletal remains deposited in outdoor environments due to numerous active processes, such as animal activity. To correctly interpret disarticulation and dispersal patterns the application of archaeological methods is vital so that valuable contextual information can be documented. In addition, when dispersal patterns are correctly interpreted, there will be a higher probability of delineating scene boundaries, locating additional skeletal elements, locating the primary depositional site of scattered remains, locating secondary depositional sites of scattered remains, and determining the original position of the body. The more common postmortem modifications that can disarticulate, modify or damage, and disperse skeletal remains include weathering, carnivore activity, rodent gnawing, botanical activity, and postmortem fractures due to improper excavation techniques. The following taphonomic processes are described to assist the forensic archaeologist in interpreting and reconstructing the scene.

3.5.2.2 Weathering

After a body is skeletonized, the remaining hard tissues will break down at a much slower rate. The destruction of bone is the result of numerous mechanical and chemical forces that include weathering. The processes of weathering can result in modifications to bone such as soil staining, sun bleaching, cracking and flaking, and eroding of skeletal elements. According to Behrensmeyer, bone weathering is defined as "the process by which the original microscopic organic and inorganic components of bone are separated from each other and destroyed by physical and chemical agents operating on the bone *in situ*, either on the surface or within the soil zone" (1978: 153). The critical factor with weathering appears to be time, but the relationship between time and weathering is not straightforward (Lyman, 1994).

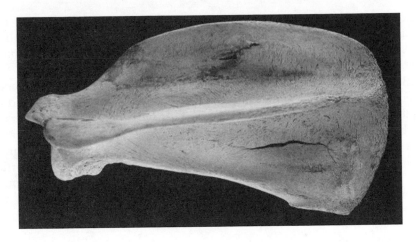

Figure 3.3 Dog scapula showing sun bleaching and weathering.

Although buried bones weather, they weather at a much slower rate than exposed bones on the surface.

Skeletal remains that have been exposed to an outdoor environment for a minimal time period may display early signs of weathering such as sun bleaching and soil staining (Figure 3.3). Continued exposure of bone leads to cracking, exfoliation, and erosion of the surfaces of skeletal elements (Figure 3.4). Although burying a body does not stop weathering, it significantly

Figure 3.4 Close-up of bone surface demonstrating advanced weathering (exfoliation and cracking of bone surface).

reduces its effect (Behrensmeyer, 1978). As the acidity, clay content, and moisture content increase in the soil, bone degradation will increase, leading to generalized erosion of skeletal elements. Preservation of skeletal remains is most favorable in dry, alkaline, sandy soils.

Bone survivability and the effects of weather can be related to differences in density due to the size of the bone, the type of bone, the age of the individual, and the nutritional and pathological status of the individual. Smaller bones will weather more quickly than larger ones due to a higher surface-to-volume ratio. The bones of a juvenile or an older individual with osteoporosis will degrade much more quickly than a healthy adult with normal bone density. Cortical bone has a higher degree of survivability than cancellous bone. For example, the ends of long bones are comprised of spongy cancellous bone and will weather more quickly than the shaft, which is comprised of dense cortical bone.

3.5.2.3 *Carnivore Activity*

It is fairly common to find animal damage on human skeletal remains that have been deposited in an outdoor setting, including both surface and shallow burials. Animal involvement results in modifications and consumption of soft tissue and bone, as well as disarticulation and dispersal of body parts. The most frequently reported canids that are responsible for scavenging human remains are dogs and coyotes (see Haglund et al., 1988; Rossi et al., 1994). Although not as frequent, the forensic literature discusses modifications to bone by scavenging from other animals, including bears (Carson et al., 2000), felines (including house cats), alligators, sharks (Iscan and McCabe, 1995; Rathbun and Rathbun, 1984), and pigs (Berryman, 2002). Each type of animal will produce its own unique modifications and patterns of damage.

The four types of carnivore tooth marks (refer to canid and rodent dental comparison in Figure 3.5) have been described in the taphonomy literature (Binford, 1981; Haglund et al., 1988; Haynes, 1980; Maguire et al., 1980), and include conical punctures, pitting, scoring, and furrows. Punctures (Figure 3.6b) are oval defects resulting from bone collapsing under the force of a single tooth cusp or canine. Conversely, pits (Figure 3.6a) are indentations that are due to a failure of the teeth to puncture the cortical surface. Scoring or striations are scratches on the surface of long bone shafts, usually perpendicular to the long axis of the bone, resulting from the teeth being dragged over the bone. Finally, furrows are deeper channels when compared with scratches and are generally located on the spongy ends of the bones (Figure 3.7). The furrows are a result of chewing by the cusps of cheek teeth, and extreme furrowing results in scooping out or hollowing out significant portions of the cancellous bone tissue from the epiphyseal end of long bones.

When carnivores chew or gnaw on long bones, they begin first on the ends of the bones where the softer cancellous bone is located and then progressively reduce the size of the shaft (Figure 3.8). Gnawing is recognized as a crenulated or ragged edge on the ends of thick long bone shafts (Binford, 1981; Maguire et al., 1980) and other bones that have been chewed (Figure 3.9). To the inexperienced eye, carnivore modifications can be confused

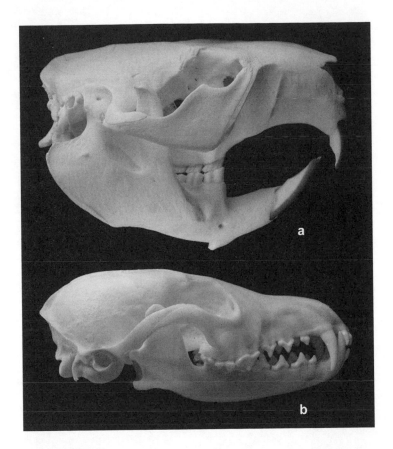

Figure 3.5 Comparison between rodent ([a] beaver) and canid ([b] red fox) dentition. (Not to scale.)

with sharp force trauma. A common way to differentiate between the two types of trauma is to look at the cross-sectional shape of the defect. Sharp force trauma will have more of a V-shaped cross-sectional shape, whereas carnivore modifications on bone (for example, from pits and scoring) will more commonly have a U-shaped cross-sectional shape.

3.5.2.4   Rodent Gnawing

All rodents share a dentition that is highly specialized for gnawing (refer to canid and rodent dental comparison in Figure 3.5). The process of gnawing is "a type of incisive movement capable of reducing hard fibrous substances in which the separated material is not always ingested" (Moore, 1981: 177). Rodents are distinguished by the presence of a hypertrophied pair of ever-growing upper and lower central incisors. Enamel is only present on the anterior and anterolateral surfaces of the incisors. As a result of this unique dental characteristic, differential wear of the harder enamel and softer dentine produces a sharp, chisel-like beveled edge (Carleton, 1984).

Figure 3.6   Canine pits (a) and puncture marks (b) on a nonhuman scapula produced by the canine teeth of a carnivore.

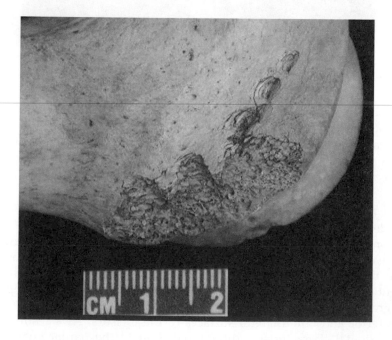

Figure 3.7   Furrowing on a nonhuman bone produced by the cheek teeth of a carnivore.

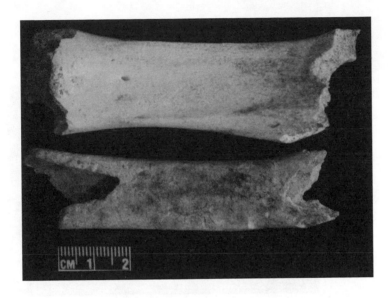

Figure 3.8 Example of two nonhuman long bones showing reduction from both ends due to carnivore chewing.

Figure 3.9 Ragged or crenulated edge created by carnivore gnawing (details shown in inset).

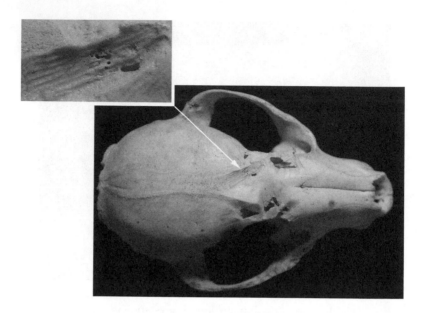

Figure 3.10   Concentrated rodent gnaw marks on a raccoon cranium (details shown in inset).

Rodents do not have lateral incisors or canines, which leaves a gap (called a diastema) between the incisors and molars. In addition, rodents also have a unique jaw joint that is loose in nature, allowing the lower jaw to move forward and backward to facilitate gnawing and chewing (Carleton, 1984; Moore, 1981).

Rodents will modify remains in varying postmortem periods, including fresh bodies, mummified bodies, and dry and fresh bone, and they have also been noted to be vectors of transport (Haglund, 1997a). It is common to find gnaw marks on bone deposited in an outdoor context. Rodents must continually gnaw hard fibrous objects, such as bone, to prevent their incisors from growing too long. Gnaw marks are recognized as patterns of shallow, parallel channels, or furrows, as shown in Figure 3.10. The adjacent linear and shallow pattern of the channels can be easily differentiated from the more irregular furrows from carnivore damage. Also, the width of the channel may provide general clues as to the size of the rodent (Hillson, 1986).

3.5.2.5   Botanical Activity

Plant activity can have profound effects on the survivability and dispersal of skeletal remains. Two of the more common botanical effects on the outer surface of bones are a green staining caused by algae growth and a brown staining caused by plant decomposition. Prolonged contact between bone and roots can result in etching on the bone surface. Etching is recognized as a dendritic pattern of shallow grooving on the surface of bones (Figure 3.11). The roots of many plants secrete humic acid and the grooves "are interpreted as the result of dissolution by acids associated with the growth and decay of roots

Figure 3.11 Dendritic (root) etching pattern with adhered roots shown on the outer surface of a cranium.

or fungus in direct contact with bone surfaces" (Behrensmeyer, 1978: 154). It is also possible to observe etching on bone due to pine needles. Pine needles are highly acidic and tend to mark the bone surface as they decompose, leaving an unorganized pattern of shallow linear etching. Plant roots can also destroy bone by perforating the cortex and growing into and within bone, resulting in additional mechanical damage. For example, it is common to find roots growing through holes in the skull such as the orbits and the nasal aperture.

3.5.2.6 Additional Taphonomic Processes That Can Damage Bone

The application of improper archaeological techniques can result not only in the loss of valuable contextual information, but may also result in extensive postmortem damage to skeletal remains. Even when proper archaeological methods are used, care must also be taken to minimize postmortem destruction when excavating remains with extensive weathering and root destruction due to their brittle nature. It may be possible to leave postmortem marks on bone that can be the result of trowel use during excavation, careless stepping on bones, or a probe penetrating the bone surface during the search for buried remains. Poor packaging of bones can also result in postmortem fractures during transport. It is important for the forensic anthropologist to distinguish postmortem damage from perimortem trauma because a trowel mark can easily be confused as sharp force trauma. In these instances, differentiating postmortem trauma is possible by an experienced forensic anthropologist because the defect of recently broken postmortem fractures will be lighter than the outer cortex of the bone and it will usually display a rough or ragged margin. Conversely, bones that are broken when they are fresh exhibit fracture surfaces that are the same color as the outer bone surface, the fracture margin usually exhibits a smooth surface, and the

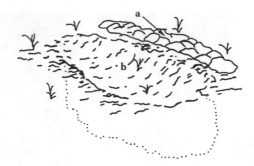

Figure 3.12   (a) Burial showing mounding of excess dirt left over from the burial digging process; and (b) a primary burial depression.

fractures can sometimes exhibit varying degrees of plastic deformation (permanently deformed). Analysis and interpretation of bone fractures should be left to the experienced forensic anthropologist.

3.5.3   Locating Burials

A burial is much more difficult to locate than a surface deposit because in most cases the body was buried to conceal its location. In many instances, it may be impossible to find a hidden burial without information providing the exact area where a body was deposited. When searching for a hidden burial, surface indicators may be the best clues used to locate a burial. A variety of surface changes may be present at the burial site when the body is buried and additional surface indicators may develop over time. In some cases, when a body is buried, the backfill from the original hole may not be placed back into the burial, therefore leaving excess piles of soil around the grave (Figure 3.12). Furthermore, a mound of soil may be present over the top of the burial as a result of soil displacement by the body, and because the soil volume changes when it is removed from its undisturbed state. Conversely, extra holes may be dug around the burial in order to cover up a body that was buried at a shallow depth. Additional surface changes that result from digging the burial include localized soil color changes due to the mixing of different colored soil horizons, a localized area that lacks vegetation when the surrounding area has vegetation, and a depressed area. A primary burial depression will occur from compaction of the loose soil that was placed over the body and collapsing of the thorax and abdominal areas during decomposition (Figure 3.12). Furthermore, smaller secondary depressions may result from additional soil compaction and soft tissue decomposition.

The combination of loosening of the soil and the presence of nutrients released into the soil from the decomposition process may promote increased vegetation growth directly over the burial (Figure 3.13a). This vegetation

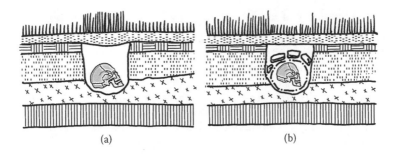

(a)   (b)

Figure 3.13   Examples of localized vegetation growth (a) and stunting (b) over a burial.

may also appear to be a more vibrant green color due to the increase of nutrients in the soil. On the other hand, there can be a noticeable decrease in vegetation growth over the burial because the vegetation has been disturbed during the burial process. Additionally, vegetation growth may be stunted if the nutrients from the decomposing body do not reach the plant roots (Figure 3.13b). This may occur due to a number of factors such as wrapping the body, materials being placed over the body, or the body being buried very deep.

It may also be possible to locate burials that animals have scavenged. There is a higher probability that animals will detect and scavenge shallow burials than deep ones because it may be difficult for them to detect the decomposition odor from a deep burial. Therefore, it may be possible to locate disturbed burials from evidence of animals digging (Figure 3.14), and from skeletal elements and personal artifacts that were brought to the ground surface

Figure 3.14   Holes (indicated by arrows) created by animals scavenging from a controlled pig burial.

Table 3.3 A Summary of Indicators That May Be Used to Locate Buried Bodies

Skeletal remains and soft tissue brought to the surface
Clothing or personal effects
Evidence of animal digging and scavenging
Abandoned tools or weapons
Soil or vegetation disturbances (e.g., growth, color changes, and lack of growth)
Depressions, soil disturbances, or unnatural mounding of soil
Soil coloration changes from mixing soil layers
Decomposition odor
Decreased soil compaction
Areas where bushes or tree limbs have been moved to conceal something buried

by scavenging. In special circumstances, digging tools and/or weapons that may have been discarded or accidentally left behind by an assailant, may be useful for locating a burial. Finally, suspicious areas where brush and tree branches may have been purposefully moved to conceal a burial should always be inspected. See Table 3.3 for indicators used to locate burials.

Cadaver dogs can also be invaluable during searches for burials by locating bodies through the detection of decomposition odor. However, a cadaver dog may only locate an area near where a body is buried and not the exact spot. This may be due to environmental factors that carry the decomposition odor to another location (see section 3.6). In this example, it is important to search an area spreading out from where the dog indicated, using traditional search methods and also trying to determine where the decomposition odor may have originated.

3.6   Cadaver Dogs

The purpose of this section is to educate anyone requiring the assistance of a cadaver dog team for a body search. It is important to understand the capabilities and limitations of cadaver dogs (or human remains detector dogs, HRD) and their handlers when choosing and working with a team during a body search. This section is not about tips for training cadaver dogs. Please, see Rebmann et al. (2000) for an excellent reference on choosing and training cadaver dogs.

3.6.1   What Is a Cadaver Dog?

Cadaver dogs (*Canis familiaris*) are used to locate human cadavers and body parts by detecting the scent of human decomposition. They are conditioned to give their handlers an alert when they detect odors associated with human decomposition and to ignore other odors including scents associated with nonhuman animal decomposition (Figure 3.15). Cadaver dogs can be trained to recognize and alert to a variety of decomposition by-products such as gases, liquids, acids, adipocere, and the musty odor from mummified tissue

Figure 3.15 Human remains search dog Ruger, with master canine trainer Mary Peter. In (a) Ruger is searching while on a leash — this allows for a more detailed search in particular areas; and (b) shows Ruger searching a defined area without a leash.

(Rebmann et al., 2000), and can provide assistance locating buried bodies, disarticulated bodies, bodies submerged in water, or hidden in vehicles or structures (Lowy and McAlhany, 2000). They will alert to bodies with a short postmortem interval, bodies that lack any signs of decomposition, decomposing bodies, skeletal remains, or even to soil containing human skeletal remains (Rebmann et al., 2000).

Dogs detect human remains when scent molecules are dispersed into the air and register a sensory reaction in the brain that is recognized by the canine. Rebmann et al. (2000) discuss the basic principles of scent cone distortion that are important to understand when conducting searches (see Table 3.4). The decomposition molecules that are shed by the object form

Table 3.4 The Principle of Scent Cone Presence and Distortion

The scent cone forms a scent pool above and around the remains

An air scent cone can be formed away from the source of the odor in the direction
of the wind

The scent can be moved away from the source along scent conduits (e.g., gravity,
surface or underground waterways, erosion or drainage patterns)

A secondary scent cone remote from the remains can form when wind or water
flow is altered by scent barriers

Scent cone distortions or breaks can form from variable wind patterns

Scent voids may develop near the remains at the dog-nose level from water flow
near the body or from elevation of the body (e.g., a body hanging from a tree)

Source: Adapted from Rebmann et al., 2000.

a primary scent cone around the decomposing body with stagnant and
unmoving air (Figure 3.16a). With wind, the scent cone will become more
and more dispersed further from the decomposing body (Figure 3.16b).
Many factors that can alter or distort scent cones, including terrain, vegetation, climate, season, and weather, can affect the position of the scent cone
in relation to the position of the body. For example, scent molecules of a
decomposing body on the ground surface or buried can be carried away
from the body by draining ground water and reappear in areas remote from

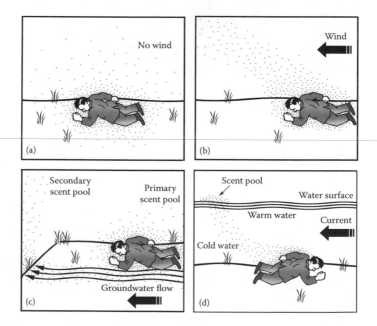

Figure 3.16   Distribution of decomposition scent cone in different environments: (a)
surface decomposition with no wind; (b) surface decomposition with wind; (c) decomposition with the scent cone being transferred to another location and by groundwater;
and (d) decomposition under water. (Adapted from Rebmann et al., 2000.)

Table 3.5 Summary of the Limitations of Cadaver Dogs

Whether the remains are actually present within the search area
Whether remains are creating a scent pool and a scent cone above ground
Air movement between the scent pool and the dog
Temperature (above freezing and below approximately 90°F/32°C)
Whether the handler guides the dog to the correct area
Whether the handler correctly interprets the dog's behavior

Source: Adapted from Rebmann et al., 2000.

the body (Figure 3.16c). In this example, the cadaver dog can indicate the presence of a buried body or surface deposition at a remote location. In addition, cadaver dogs can detect bodies submerged in water because the decomposition odor of the body will be carried to the surface of the water. However, water currents can carry the scent of a submerged decomposing body to another location away from the remains, leaving a scent void on the surface of the water above the body (Figure 3.16d).

3.6.2 Limitations of Cadaver Dogs

A successful search using cadaver dogs depends on numerous factors including the presearch investigation, type of search, the handler's skills, weather during the search, the terrain of the search area, the circumstances leading to death and deposition of the body, and the time since death (Rebmann et al., 2000). Table 3.5 provides a summary of the limitations of cadaver dogs and scent detection for body searches. Furthermore, the dog's ability to pinpoint the exact location of a buried body depends on decomposition odor reaching the surface. Decomposition odor may not reach the ground surface if the depth of the body is too deep, if the soil type is not permeable enough, and if the body is wrapped in material that will not release the odor. The soil may need to be vented when a cadaver dog is not able to locate a suspected burial in a given area or when a dog does not indicate the exact location of a buried body. The search area can be vented with a T-bar probe (see Section 3.7.1 in this chapter) to bring decomposition odor to the ground surface. Rebmann et al. (2000) suggest venting every 18 inches or 46 cm utilizing grid lines and offsetting the line of holes in each line.

3.6.3 Finding a Cadaver Dog

Although there is an obvious need for cadaver dogs or human remains detector (HRD) dogs, they have been minimally represented in the law enforcement canine population across the United States, and smaller law enforcement agencies may not have their own team (Lowy and McAlhany, 2000). The canine HRD specialty has not been given the same attention as dogs that are trained in the explosive and narcotic specialties since it may not be feasible to include another canine specialty in smaller law enforcement agencies for the occasional search. Smaller agencies can usually request the services of a larger nearby department, thereby justifying not having a cadaver dog program. When agencies seek the assistance of an HRD team, it is essential to determine their level of expertise because the abilities of teams vary. It is important to ask questions about team qualifications including training, certifications, and the number of cases handled (Lowy and McAlhany, 2000). Recommendations of teams throughout your state can be provided by various state law enforcement agencies or the FBI.

3.7 Intrusive Search Methods

After the nonintrusive search techniques have been exhausted, there are a number of intrusive techniques that can be used to further explore areas identified previously as areas of interest. It should be remembered that intrusive methods will ultimately destroy the site, so the decision to use them must be made carefully.

3.7.1 Probe Searches

The most common intrusive search method is using a probe to locate a clandestine grave and the outline of the grave itself. Numerous authors have discussed the effectiveness of using probes to locate forensic and archaeological graves (Boyd, 1979; Imaizumi, 1974; Killam, 1990; Morse et al., 1983; Owsley, 1995). This method should be used systematically across a search grid and can also be used as a follow-up method after a visual search to further inspect suspicious areas.

The most common probe used is called a T-bar probe. Probing is conducted by pushing a pointed metal or fiberglass rod, typically 4 feet (1.2 m) in length and 5/16 to 1/2 in (approximately 1 to 1.5 cm) in diameter with a crossbar handle at the top (Figure 3.17), into the ground at regular intervals within a search grid. This method is used to determine the qualitative differences in density of subsurface materials, because the disturbed soil of the grave will be less dense than the surrounding undisturbed soil. When using equal amounts of pressure, the probe will penetrate much farther into disturbed soil than it does into undisturbed soil. As individuals work their way through the grid, soft spots or areas where the probe easily penetrates the soil compared with the compacted surrounding subsurface, are noted and marked for further investigation

Another type of probe that can be used in forensic investigation is a penetrometer, more commonly used for agricultural applications. A penetrometer has a pressure gauge at the junction of the rod with the crossbar (Figure 3.18) that measures soil compactness by providing a quantitative measurement. Since probing is based on relative and subjective resistance, it should be conducted by a single person if time permits. With practice in the given search area, an individual can get a good idea of the amount of pressure needed to probe a specific depth.

The third type of probe is a soil-coring probe, useful for determining whether soil horizons have been mixed. (This probe is not used to determine whether the soil compactness has changed, but is used to determine whether

Figure 3.17   Author John Schultz demonstrates the use of a T-bar probe to detect differences in soil compaction in a depressed area.

soil horizons are mixed.) This is done by removing and examining a vertical core of soil. A soil-coring probe is generally 3 to 4 feet (0.9 to 1.2 m) in length, and the end that is inserted into the ground has a hollow tube to collect soil that is 1/2 to 3/4 in (around 1 cm) in diameter and 7 to 9 in (17 to 23 cm) in length (Figure 3.19). One side of the coring section is open so the stratigraphy (layers)

Figure 3.18   Use of a penetrometer probe with a gauge to show differences in soil compaction.

Figure 3.19   Author John Schultz demonstrates the use of a probe with soil corer to detect the presence of undisturbed or disturbed soil horizons: (a) soil core showing natural horizons; and (b) soil core showing mottled or mixed soil horizons.

of the soil can be viewed. Once a core of the natural stratigraphy is determined (Figure 3.19a), disturbed soil will be recognized as having a mottled appearance (Figure 3.19b) produced from the mixing of the soil horizons. An advantage of this method over standard probes is that it is not pushed into the ground as far and there is less of a chance of damaging the body and evidence.

If a probe is going to be used as a primary search instrument, a grid should be placed over the search area. Grid lines should be placed close enough together so the buried item in question will not be missed between two adjacent lines. Depending on the size of a buried body, grid intervals should be placed anywhere from 2 to 3 feet (approximately 35 cm to 1 m) apart. There should be one person using the probe and one person taking notes and marking a scaled map of the search area. The individual using the probe should indicate to the note taker whether the soil is more or less compacted. Pin flags should be carefully placed in the areas that require further evaluation. After the initial search is finished, additional probing should be undertaken in suspicious areas at smaller intervals.

3.7.2   Disadvantages of Using Probe Searches

Some inherent difficulties do exist in using the soil probe method. It is not normally a search method that is used systematically over large areas because it can be time consuming. In cases in which sandy soils are present, it may not be possible to reliably sample differences between disturbed and undisturbed soil. If the probe is pushed into the ground too far, it may damage bones and other evidence in the burial. Furthermore, any damage to the body or bones may be incorrectly interpreted as perimortem trauma.

3.8   Shovel Testing and Shovel Shining

Although invasive testing with a shovel is not a recommended search method, there are cases when this may be the only alternative after other search methods are exhausted or as a follow-up to a visual search. There are two ways to use a shovel when trying to locate or delineate the boundaries of a grave. The first method is digging a test pit in an attempt to locate evidence of a burial or a body. In this instance, a small test hole is dug with a spade shovel, and all removed soil should be screened so that no potential evidence is missed. However, we caution that this should be used as a last alternative because it is very destructive.

If there are possible indicators of a burial, a sharpened flat edge shovel (not a spade shovel) may be used to delineate the boundaries of the burial feature. When removing soil, the proper method is to shave the surface by using a skimming motion, also known as shovel shining (Figure 3.20). This method does not involve digging, only the removal of small amounts of soil in centimeter depths, so that if the outline of a grave appears it will not be missed (Figure 3.21).

Figure 3.20   Orange County Sheriff's Office homicide detective Dave Clarke (left) and authors Lana Williams (center) and Sandra Wheeler (right) shovel shining a test excavation while searching for a buried body at a forensic scene.

Figure 3.21   Grave outline revealed after shovel shining.

3.9   Forensic Backhoe

Most forensic anthropologists have heard the obligatory story of law enforcement using a backhoe to excavate a burial. For obvious reasons, such as considerable damage to a burial, skeletal remains or evidence, a backhoe is not an ideal piece of equipment to use for a forensic search. However, in certain instances, a backhoe, having a flat blade without teeth on the bucket or an elevated scraper, may be a last alternative in searching when all other methods have been exhausted, or when it may not be possible to use traditional methods (Figure 3.22). This method has been used in archaeology to locate burials by scraping the sterile topsoil to expose the location of grave sites (Bass, 1963; Ubelaker, 1989). One advantage of using a backhoe is that it can remove a considerable amount of soil in a short period of time. Finally, a backhoe may be the only realistic option in areas where traditional search methods may not work, such as landfills or heavily flooded areas.

A bulldozer should not be used because it can significantly damage any evidence as well as the search area. Since a bulldozer pushes the soil around, there is a greater chance of mixing soil horizons in addition to damaging evidence from the metal tracks driving over and compressing the survey area. On the other hand, when a backhoe or scraper is used, it can extend the bucket over a small area so the heavy equipment will not damage material by driving over it. An experienced operator can control the machine so that the surface is removed a few inches at a time, leaving a smooth surface behind (Bass, 1963; Bass and Birkby, 1978; Ubelaker, 1989). There should be someone guiding the backhoe operator and checking the ground after it has been scraped to determine whether a burial has appeared, and also someone checking the removed soil for any evidence. If possible, it is recommended to have someone familiar with human skeletal remains at the scene assisting

Figure 3.22   A forensic "backhoe" (Caterpiller 320B trackhoe excavator with extended boom) being used to search for a suspected location of a buried car containing two bodies.

with the search. As the ground is scraped, workers should be looking for differences in color changes in relation to the surrounding undisturbed soil. The soil in the grave is generally a different color due to mixing of the soil horizons and decomposition products. Once anything suspicious is located in the area being scraped, all work with the backhoe must cease, and less destructive methods should then be used to determine whether a burial is present.

chapter 4

GPR and Other Geophysical Search Technologies

Another option for searches is to use geophysical prospecting methods. A geophysical survey in a forensic context is important not only in locating buried bodies and forensic evidence; it is equally as important when clearing suspected areas so law enforcement can direct investigations elsewhere. Geophysical prospecting is the study of locating and mapping hidden objects or features that are underground or underwater. In most instances, geophysical prospecting methods are nonintrusive or nondestructive. In other words, one advantage of using geophysical technology for forensic and archaeological ground searches is preservation of the scene or site since the ground is not disturbed. Geophysical prospecting can be used as a follow-up technique to searching potential areas after a visual search has been conducted, as well as in isolating smaller areas for further investigation. Finally, one of the main advantages of geophysical prospecting methods is that they can be used to search areas where traditional search methods cannot be used, such as over concrete and pavement. For example, the survey can be performed over a house foundation without any initial destruction to the slab. If there are potential areas that need further investigation under the slab, there will be only minimal destruction because the exact areas to search will have been highlighted during the geophysical survey.

The purpose of a geophysical survey is to detect anomalies that are recognized as localized areas of contrasting properties, such as a buried metallic weapon in the soil (see Table 4.1 for a summary of geophysical technologies and their uses). In this case, the buried metallic weapon may be detected with geophysical instrumentation because it would have different electrical properties (that is, higher conductivity) than the surrounding soil. However, the only way to determine what produces the anomaly is to then use a destructive follow-up method such as probing or excavating. Geophysical prospecting methods can be classified into two basic types: passive and active (Reynolds, 1997). Both methods involve measuring signals that are either natural or induced. Active methods use technology that sends an induced signal into the ground by a transmitter and then measures the returning signal via a receiver

Table 4.1 The Applications and Disadvantages of Different Geophysical Technologies (see Table 4.2 for information regarding GPR)

Geophysical Technology	Applications	Disadvantages
Conductivity meters*	Metallic weapons and other large metallic objects May find burials	Expensive Requires expertise
Resistivity meters*	Metallic weapons and other large metallic objects May find burials	Moderately priced Requires minimal ground disturbance
Magnetometers	Metallic weapons and metal objects	Expensive Requires expertise
Metal detectors	Metallic weapons and metal objects	Only detects small objects at shallow depths
Magnetic locators	Metallic weapons and metal objects	Only detects small objects at shallow depths
Side-Scan sonar	Water searches	Expensive Requires expertise

* These technologies may not be useful for detecting burials due to insufficient contrast between the burial and the undisturbed surrounding soil. We suggest these technologies be used for grave searches only in cases in which GPR cannot be used.

in the instrument. Conversely, passive methods only contain a receiver that measures variations within the natural fields of the earth, such as gravitational and magnetic fields, that are generally produced by buried metallic objects.

The following description of geophysical tools is not an exhaustive list of every tool that has been used for forensic and archaeological applications. The purpose of this chapter is to discuss the best equipment that may be available to search for buried bodies and metallic forensic evidence in various contexts and to explain how the equipment works and should be used. The list reviews only the more common equipment that has been used for forensic and archaeological surveys such as ground-penetrating radar (GPR), conductivity meters, resistivity meters, magnetometers, metal detectors, magnetic locators, and side-scan sonar. Of all these technologies, ground-penetrating radar will be the best option when searching for buried bodies if the local environmental and geographical conditions are suitable. However, if it is not possible to use GPR because local conditions are not appropriate, equipment is not available, or the search is for small metallic evidence, then another of the geophysical methods described in this chapter may be useful.

4.1   Ground-Penetrating Radar

Ground-penetrating radar has proven to be the best geophysical tool to use for burial searches in archaeological, forensic, and controlled contexts. For example, GPR has become a valuable search tool used to locate or verify the location of historic or archaeological graves (Bevan, 1991; Davis and Annan, 1989; Davis et al., 1998; King et al., 1993; Vaughn, 1986) and it has been used to locate an increasing number of forensic bodies that have been interred for differing postmortem intervals and in varying environments (Calkin et al., 1995; Davenport, 2001a; Hunter, 1996b; Mellett, 1992; Nobes, 2000; Reynolds, 1997). At the same time, controlled studies using buried pig cadavers have demonstrated that GPR is the most effective geophysical prospecting tool used to delineate graves (France et al., 1992; France et al., 1997).

4.1.1 GPR Equipment

The most common GPR units available from commercial manufacturers employ pulsed radar energy of one center frequency. Standard GPR systems consist of four main elements: the control unit, the transmitting unit (Tx), the receiving unit (Rx), and the display unit. GPR systems used in archaeology and forensics usually use monostatic antennas; the transmitter and receiver are contained within the same antenna housing. GPR antennas come in standard frequencies that are designated by the frequency corresponding to the peak power of the radiated spectrum, or the center frequency. Antenna choice is a compromise between penetration depth and subsurface resolution. Lower frequency antennae (for example, 300-MHz) are used for much deeper surveys, but have a lower resolution of small subsurface targets. In some instances, a higher resolution antenna (for example, 900-MHz) may yield so much detail or clutter (i.e., small discontinuities that reflect energy but are not the target of the survey) that the target may not be readily identified (Nobes, 2000; Schultz et al., 2002; Schultz, 2003). Antennae with frequencies from 400-MHz to 500-MHz are appropriate for forensic and archeological applications because they provide an excellent compromise between depth of penetration and resolution of subsurface features (Schultz et al., 2002; Schultz, 2003).

GPR equipment can be configured a number of different ways for use in the field. The first option is to have the antenna and control unit separate from one another, where one individual pulls the antenna across each transect on a grid while another individual monitors the GPR imagery on the control unit and directs the antenna operator. The second option has one individual pulling the antenna and operating a control unit that is attached to the body via a harness (Figure 4.1). The newest option that is offered from most manufacturers is to mount the antenna and control unit on a cart that can be operated by one individual (Figure 4.2).

Operating the GPR begins with placing the antenna on, or near, the ground surface and then moving it over the area being surveyed. GPR is an active tool that emits continuous electromagnetic pulses of short duration that propagate from the transmitting unit in the antenna downward into the ground. As the signal penetrates into the subsurface, it will be reflected, refracted, and scattered as it encounters materials of contrasting electrical properties (Figure 4.3). The receiving portion of the antenna records the returning signal and sends it back to the control unit along a different line

Figure 4.1   Author John Schultz demonstrating how the GPR is operated when one individual is pulling the 500-MHz antenna with the monitor secured to the body via a shoulder harness.

located within the cable. The control unit amplifies and formats the raw, reflected signal for immediate display on a video monitor or for paper print-out. GPR files can also be downloaded to an external computer to be stored for further viewing and for postprocessing the data to increase resolution of the imagery using a variety of commercially available software programs.

Large or small features are generally detected by GPR due to increases in conductivity and voids. For example, conductivity increases can be due

Figure 4.2   Author John Schultz demonstrating how the GPR is operated when using a survey cart with the 500-MHz antenna secured to the bottom of the cart.

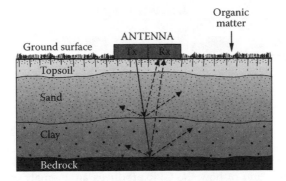

Figure 4.3 Generalized soil profile with transmitted radar waves from the GPR that have been reflected and scattered as they encounter horizon interfaces of differing electrical (conductivity) properties.

to an increase in cations or moisture in certain soils or stratigraphic horizons such as clay. Conductivity increases also occur with buried metallic objects and buried electric lines. There are a number of features to recognize on a GPR profile (Figure 4.4). When a subsurface feature is detected by GPR, it is called a reflection or anomaly, which can be produced from features that may be described as either a "point source" or planar surface (Conyers and Goodman, 1997). Point sources, or small hyperbolic reflections, are more commonly referred to as anomalies and are due to smaller features such as tunnels, voids, pipes, graves, buried bodies, small archaeological features,

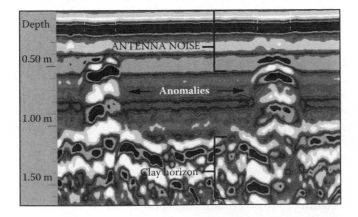

Figure 4.4 GPR profile of two pig cadavers buried at approximately 60 cm. The profile shows two anomalies from the buried pig cadavers, the bottom of the profile is demarcated by a clay horizon, and the top of the profile is horizontal banding from the antenna noise.

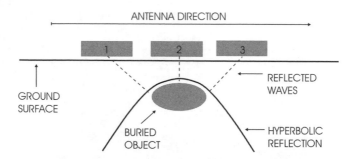

Figure 4.5   Illustration of how the GPR produces an anomaly. A point source or anomaly is generated from one single subsurface feature due to the wide angle of the transmitted radar beam. The hyperbolic characteristics of the anomaly are due to the increased travel time of the radar signal before and after the subsurface feature is detected.

and weapons (Figure 4.4). Planar surfaces, conversely, can be due to interfaces of stratigraphic horizons (for example, sand, clay, loam), water tables, or large archaeological features, such as floors and foundations. In addition, at the top of the profile is prominent horizontal banding, or antenna noise (Figure 4.4), that appears in most GPR profiles (Shih and Doolittle, 1984; Sternberg and McGill, 1995). If the banding obscures the GPR profile, it can be removed using postprocessing software.

Point sources are visible on the GPR printout and are produced from the wide angle of the transmitted radar pulse that is in the shape of an elliptical cone. The long axis of the ellipse is parallel to the direction that the antenna travels, and the radiation pattern on a horizontal plane is directed below the antenna, as well as in front, behind, and to the sides as it travels across the ground surface (Conyers and Goodman, 1997). Therefore, as the antenna is dragged over a subsurface object, it will detect the object prior to arriving directly over it, as well as when it is directly over it, and will continue to detect the subsurface object after passing it (Figure 4.5). When the point source is detected prior to and after the antenna has passed, it is recorded as if the point source is directly beneath the antenna, but the travel time to the object is increased. The hyperbolic characteristics of the anomalies are due to the increased travel time of the radar signal before and after the subsurface feature is detected.

4.1.2   *Advantages and Disadvantages of GPR*

There are many advantages for using GPR in forensic contexts. The data are displayed in real-time and the excellent resolution of subsurface features is only surpassed by side-scan sonar in water. Also, it is possible to estimate the depth of forensic targets with the potential of immediate results in the field without

Table 4.2 Advantages and Disadvantages of Using GPR for Forensic Applications

Advantages	Disadvantages
Real-time display	Expense of equipment
Immediate results in the field	Requires experienced operator
Excellent resolution	Topography must be relatively level,
Detection of graves and metallic	smooth, and open
evidence	Poor penetration in clayey and
Estimation of depth of forensic targets	saturated soils
Penetration of concrete and pavement	Slow coverage speed

postprocessing the data. GPR can be used to search for graves and large metallic evidence. In forensic contexts, GPR surveys work best in dry, sandy soils with little subsurface debris. GPR can also be used in a variety of contexts such as over concrete, pavement, and hard-packed surfaces, and although it can be used in a boat over fresh water to search for large submersed drums or vehicles, it should only be used over water if side-scan sonar is not available.

There are a number of disadvantages that will limit or prevent the use of GPR as a search tool. First, the equipment is expensive and it requires an experienced operator to interpret the data. Also, the search area must be fairly level, smooth, and open with few trees, and must have relatively few buried metal objects. A variety of buried objects will produce an anomaly similar to that of a buried body or a grave. However, experienced operators may be able to rule out specific anomalies based on their experience and the orientation of anomalies to specific features. For example, if anomalies are detected near a large tree, the tree roots may be producing the anomaly. Soil properties will also affect GPR since it may not work in saturated soils, and it may be very difficult to locate a buried body or forensic evidence in clayey soils. In addition, it may take quite a long time to perform a GPR survey depending on the size of an area. Thus, it would not be feasible to perform a GPR survey in areas that consist of many acres. Table 4.2 summarizes advantages and disadvantages of GPR use for forensic contexts.

4.2   Conductivity Meters

Conductivity is the ability of a material to transmit electricity. An active electromagnetic (EM) instrument, such as a conductivity meter, containing a transmitter and a receiver, measures differences in the electrical conductivity of the ground. The EM transmitter projects a primary electromagnetic field into the ground that will generate small eddy currents on the surface of conducting objects (ferrous and nonferrous) or features, and the eddy currents in turn create a secondary magnetic field that is measured by the receiver (Figure 4.6). The most popular EM technology for forensic and archaeological contexts is the horizontal loop or slingram method that is operated by one person (Figure 4.7). The generic unit in Figure 4.7 contains a long antenna rod

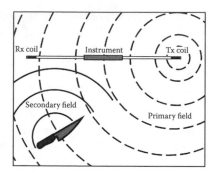

Figure 4.6　An electromagnetic field is transmitted into the ground from the transmitting coil, which generates small eddy currents on the surface of conducting objects (e.g., knife), and the eddy currents in turn create a secondary electromagnetic field that is measured by the receiver coil.

measuring 4 m (smaller models are available) with transmitting and receiving antennas mounted together at a fixed distance. The unit is operated by one person and should be carried horizontally above the ground. The slingram instrument measuring 4 m in length averages conductivity measurements to a depth of approximately 6 m. However, the highest sensitivity is for features located in the top meter of soil. Therefore, in a forensic context the EM is best suited for detecting buried metal objects at shallow depths. Measurements should be taken along a grid and electromagnetic anomalies can be plotted on a map for data interpretation. Conductivity is reported in units of siemens or millimho (mho/m) of material, and, in theory, should produce results

Figure 4.7　The slingram conductivity method in this figure consists of a long antenna pole that measures 4 m with transmitting and receiving antennas mounted at opposite ends of the pole. The unit is operated by one person and should be carried horizontally above the ground.

similar to a resistivity survey, since resistivity is the opposite of conductivity (Davenport, 2001b).

A major advantage of EM is that the unit does not have to be in contact with the ground surface (Davenport, 2001b; Reynolds, 1997). Electromagnetic instruments will detect metallic objects such as guns, knives, and other metallic evidence, and in certain instances, it might be possible to detect a grave if there is enough contrast between the backfill and undisturbed soil. Electromagnetic instruments can be used in wooded areas and over hard ground and concrete. In addition, a combination of GPR and EM can be used in large open areas because surveys can be conducted quickly with EM methods. For example, Nobes (2000) first used EM to survey a large area and then followed with GPR to locate a buried forensic body in an area that was targeted with the EM survey.

Davenport (2001b) notes a number of limitations using conductivity. One disadvantage is that the measurements produced by an EM are only averages of all ground conductivities within the depth range. Another major disadvantage of EM concerns noise created by metallic objects in the vicinity, such as cultural features (for example, fences, pipes, power lines). The operator must remove all metal items worn such as car keys, belt buckles, and steel-toed boots before conducting an EM survey. In addition, certain geologic features that have high conductivities, such as clayey soils, may dissipate the EM field signal and not permit signal penetration.

4.3   Resistivity Meters

Resistivity is the resistance of a given material to the passage of electricity; it is also the reciprocal of conductivity (Killam, 1990). The potential of a given area of the earth to conduct electricity is measured during resistivity surveys in ohms. This surveying method is based on the predictable electrical behavior exhibited in a solid medium of uniform density (Killam, 1990). Induced electrical current flows horizontally and vertically into the ground. Any measured deviations from the predicted flow of current are due to variations in the conduction medium. It is possible to estimate the location of the variations, or anomalies, because this surveying method requires placing electrodes in the ground at known distances. Measurements should be taken along a grid and anomalies can be plotted on a map for data interpretation.

There are a number of disadvantages to using resistivity for forensic applications (Killam, 1990). Resistivity works best on flat ground and is influenced by soil moisture. There can also be interference from metal and electrical sources. Anomalies of interest, such as graves, may have a low contrast with the surrounding soil and may not be detected. This method must have some type of ground contact that results in a minimal amount of surface destruction, and there will be slower coverage speed than an EM survey because electrodes must be placed in the ground.

4.4   Magnetometers

A magnetic survey is used to detect the magnetic field of ferromagnetic objects and is performed using a passive instrument called a magnetometer (MAG). MAGs do not transmit a signal into the ground and, therefore, do not have a transmitter. Instead, they have a receiver that detects the magnetic field of buried ferrous objects. There are a variety of commercial MAGs such as proton magnetometers, flux-gate magnetometers, and alkali vapor magnetometers available, and, of these, the proton magnetometer is most often used in archaeological contexts. Data are collected in the field along a grid then downloaded to a computer to be processed. Anomalies can be recognized on a contour magnetic intensity map by contrasts between the target and matrix.

A MAG survey is useful in archaeological contexts for detecting buried artifacts or features that contain ferromagnetic objects, and also in detecting buried fired-earth features such as stone hearths or fire pits. In forensic contexts, a MAG survey may be useful to detect weapons and other forensic evidence. However, it will not directly detect a grave, but may be helpful locating a buried body if ferrous materials are buried in the grave with the body. Detecting magnetic anomalies is a function of the differences in contrast due to the magnetic properties, size, shape, orientation, and distance between a ferrous object and point of measurement (Davenport, 2001b). An advantage of a MAG over a metal detector or magnetic locator is that it provides quantitative measurements that are used to create a map indicating magnetic anomalies. The major disadvantage of a MAG is interference or noise from cultural features (for example, fences, pipes, power lines, and metal debris) and geologic features in the vicinity.

Davenport (2001b) recommends using a gradient magnetometer that contains two sensors (separated by a distance usually of 2 to 3 feet, or less than a meter) for forensic contexts because this survey method has a number of advantages over a traditional MAG with one sensor. The use of two sensor heads decreases the noise from surface debris and cultural features, and provides increased resolution of subsurface features.

4.5   Metal Detectors

Metal detectors are the most common electromagnetic devices because they are relatively inexpensive and easy to use compared with other equipment, and they are very popular with law enforcement and hobbyists (Figure 4.8). Metal detectors are electromagnetic devices that operate on the same principle as electromagnetic surveying equipment. The antenna head or search coil contains transmitting and receiving coils. An electromagnetic field is transmitted into the ground from the transmitting coil in the immediate vicinity of the search head (Figure 4.9). The field enters conducting objects and creates tiny circulating eddy currents across their surfaces. The eddy currents receive their power from the transmitted electromagnetic field, resulting in a power loss that is detected by the instrument (Garett, 1998).

Figure 4.8 Orange County Sheriff's Office homicide detective Dave Clarke uses a metal detector during a forensic search.

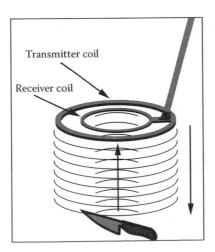

Figure 4.9 On a typical metal detector, an electromagnetic field is transmitted into the ground from the transmitter coil. When the field encounters a conducting object, such as the knife in this figure, a secondary electromagnetic field is created flowing outward into the surrounding soil and is detected by the receiver coil.

In addition, eddy currents generate a secondary electromagnetic field that flows outward into the surrounding soil and is detected by the receiver.

Metal detectors will detect conductive metals and some minerals, and the more expensive models can discriminate among different metals. The basic metal detector consists of an adjustable stem with a control box at one end and a search coil at the end toward the ground. The most popular metal detectors are very low frequency (VLF) detectors that can electronically balance out or reject, either manually or automatically, the natural mineral content of the soil or ground surface. In addition, many high-end VLF metal detectors also have discriminating capabilities that can accurately indicate the type of target and reduce the number of false positives by ignoring and not detecting signals from small iron and aluminum trash metals. Furthermore, computerized models can also be helpful in determining the precise location and depth of targets (Garett, 1998).

One of the options available with metal detectors manufactured today is the ability to change the search head for specific targets. It is important to have the correct size head when searching for specific targets. Large heads (10 to 18 in/25 to 45 cm) can penetrate deeper but only locate larger objects. Smaller objects are not detected by larger coils because they are treated as noise. Conversely, smaller heads (for example, 5 in/12 cm) are better for detecting smaller objects, but penetrate shallower depths. A good general purpose head is from 7 to 9 in (18 to 23 cm) depending on the manufacturer and type of detector, is lightweight, responds to a number of different target sizes, and has good scanning width (Garett, 1998). Other options available to increase scanning depth include depth multiplier attachments that can extend the detection depth of metal detectors and can easily attach to existing heads. Various manufacturers also offer special metal detectors called two-box systems that are designed to locate large objects (for example, buried 55-gallon drums) at much greater depths than a traditional metal detector can penetrate. A two-box system consists of separate transmitting and receiving coils that can be mounted on either end of a pole, with the complete unit measuring approximately 50 in/125 cm. Submersible search heads are also available and can be useful when searching a shallow water environment where a gun or knife may have been discarded.

Before using a metal detector, it is important to first tune the machine to local soil conditions per manufacturer directions. The use of headphones is also recommended to enhance audio perception because sound is brought directly to your ears, while simultaneously masking potential interference in noisy areas (Garett, 1998). When using the metal detector, the coil should be held in front of the operator, parallel and as close to the ground as possible for maximum coverage and depth (Figure 4.10). The coil should be moved in a sweeping motion at least one half the length of the search coil to minimize the underground area that is not covered (Figure 4.11). When operating a metal detector, there will be a pronounced audio signal and an increase in the analog or digital readout when the head passes over a buried target. The audio signal will be

Figure 4.10 When using the metal detector, the coil should be held in front of the operator, parallel and as close to the ground as possible for maximum coverage and depth.

loudest when the head is directly over the target. To pinpoint the exact location of the target, move the search coil across the area from different directions.

Metal detectors should be a piece of equipment available for most searches. Law enforcement should have a high-end metal detector with a number of different-sized coils available for searches. Metal detectors are helpful in locating shallow buried bullets, bullet casings, weapons, and other buried metallic forensic evidence. In addition, metal detectors can be useful when used in combination with more sophisticated geophysical equipment (Davenport, 2001b). They can be used prior to and after conducting magnetic,

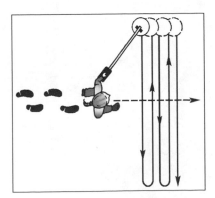

Figure 4.11 The coil of a metal detector should be moved in a sweeping motion at least one half the length of the search coil to minimize the underground area that is not covered.

electromagnetic, or GPR survey by delineating near surface objects and trash that can produce interference during a geophysical survey. Disadvantages of this method include the fact that metal detectors will not be able to directly detect a grave unless there are metal objects in the grave at a shallow enough depth to be detected. Furthermore, it will only detect small objects that are buried at very shallow and high-end computerized models will require some training before use.

4.6 *Magnetic Locators*

A less expensive option and a much easier piece of equipment to operate for locating ferromagnetic objects is a magnetic locator (also called a valve and box locator). A magnetic locator is a passive instrument that operates on a similar principle as the gradient magnetometer (section 4.4). Manufacturers design this equipment as a walking staff (usually 35 to 42 in or 89 to 106 cm in length) with a long shaft and a small control box at the top end (Figure 4.12). The shaft contains two sensors that respond to changes in magnetic fields from buried ferromagnetic objects, including metallic weapons that are in close proximity to the shaft.

The readout and sound operate very similarly to a metal detector; as you move closer to a metal target, an audible sound or digital readout will get higher. During use, the shaft should be swept from side to side in front of the operator.

Figure 4.12   Author John Schultz demonstrating the use of a magnetic locator, which is swept from side to side while searching for buried metallic objects.

A magnetic locator can locate larger objects at deep depths, such as a 55-gallon drum up to 8 feet (2.44 m) deep (Schonstedt Instrument Company, 2001). However, smaller objects can only be detected at shallow depths (Schohstedt Instrument Company, 2001). According to the manufacturer, a handgun may only be detected at depths of less than a foot (30 cm).

4.7 Side-Scan Sonar

Side-scan sonar is a marine geophysical tool that uses sound waves to produce a detailed graphic image, similar to an aerial image, of the surface of the seafloor, riverbed, or lake bottom. The system includes a torpedo-shaped towfish (Figure 4.13), a data collection control unit or computer, a tow cable, and a power supply. The towfish is towed in the water behind a boat at a depth of 10 to 20 feet (3 to 6 m) above the bottom. The side-scan sonar towfish contains a transducer with a transmitter and receiver that projects high or low frequency bursts of acoustic energy on both sides of the towfish in thin fan-shaped beams (Figure 4.14). The sound pulses or echoes, reflecting off of a relief or object projecting above the bottom surface, are received by the transducers, amplified, and transmitted up the tow cable to the graphic recorder on the survey vessel. The strength and travel time of reflected pulses are recorded and processed into an image or picture of the bottom surface.

Side-scan sonar has many uses but has become an important search tool in archaeology and forensic contexts when underwater searches are conducted. For example, side-scan sonar is routinely used to search for old shipwrecks, archaeological sites, downed aircraft, submersed vehicles, and this method has been used successfully to locate drowned victims laying on the underwater ground surface (Figure 4.15). The major advantages of sonar include: it can be used in both fresh and saltwater, it is not affected by murky or black water, it can be used in deep depths, and it also provides a representative picture of the submersed object. Disadvantages of side-scan sonar include poor detection of objects that are completely buried beneath the seafloor, and that extremely rocky or irregular bottoms can make it difficult to interpret sonar returns.

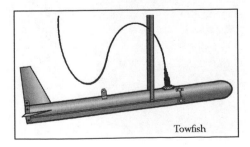

Towfish

Figure 4.13 Illustration of the side-scan sonar towfish that is dragged in the water.

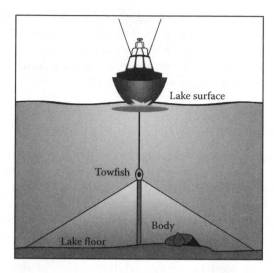

Figure 4.14   The sonar pulse from the side-scan sonar towfish is fan-shaped and is projected directly under the towfish and to either side.

4.8   How to Find a Consultant for a Geophysical Survey

It is important to note that surveys using geophysical instruments must be performed and interpreted by experienced operators. Unfortunately, the high cost of a number of geophysical tools, particularly GPR, means that it is not feasible for most law enforcement departments to own their own

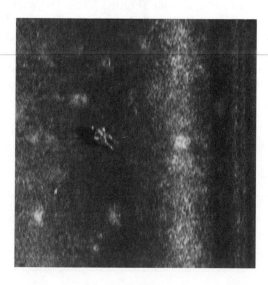

Figure 4.15   Side-scan sonar image of a drowned victim located on the bottom of a lake floor. (Photo courtesy of G. Ralston.)

equipment and that they must bring in an outside consultant to perform a survey. In most instances, GPR will be the best tool to use for body searches if site conditions are favorable for this equipment. When law enforcement is searching for a GPR operator, they can start by inquiring at local universities, environmental or archaeological firms, or alternately, conduct Internet searches. However, when bringing in a consultant, preference should be given to operators who have experience searching for small subsurface objects buried at shallow depths, such as bodies and archaeological features. Conducting a GPR survey for small subsurface objects that are routinely encountered in forensic and archaeological surveys requires additional training not only in interpreting the results, but also in setting up the grid and performing the survey. This can be a problem if the consultant only has experience searching for large geologic features because the most limiting factor when using GPR for forensic applications is the operator's experience. Also, it is important to make sure that a proper grid is used during the geophysical survey.

When selecting a consultant for a geophysical survey it is important to make inquiries about the consultant's experience and how they will conduct the geophysical survey. The investigator should be aware that for forensic geophysical surveys it is very important that a grid be setup with appropriate spacing between the transects (each line on the grid). Even if a body is buried within the survey area, it may not be detected if a controlled survey is not conducted properly. Transects need to be spaced close enough together (for example, 3 feet or 1 m transects for adults and less for smaller children) so a forensic target is not missed between transects. This method will provide 100% coverage if performed in one cardinal direction (i.e., east-to-west or north-to-south) and, if time permits, performed in both cardinal directions, which will provide 200% coverage. The best chance of success for finding a body or clearing an area will only be achieved by choosing a qualified and experienced consultant who will perform a controlled geophysical survey.

chapter 5

The Collection of Botanical and Entomological Evidence

Within the United States and around the world, forensic entomologists and forensic botanists are being called upon with increasing frequency as important members of police investigations and medico-legal investigation teams. When properly collected, preserved, and analyzed by an experienced and trained team member, insect and plant evidence gathered from and around human remains can provide some of the most valuable information concerning the victim's death. In particular, both can provide important information in determining time since death or postmortem interval (PMI). We recognize that experts in these areas of specialization are not always readily available to assist in crime scene recovery, so the aim of this chapter is to familiarize the reader with appropriate procedures for the identification and recovery of such evidence to assist an expert in interpreting the evidence at a later date.

5.1 Forensic Botany

The application of botany to crime scene investigation is a relatively recent development, emerging as a science in the early 1980s (Mildenhall, 1982). Forensic botany is the application of information gleaned from plants to answer questions in legal investigations (Bates et al., 1997; Bock and Norris, 1995; 1997; Hall 1988; 1997; Mildenhall 1982; 1988; 1990; 1992; Miller Coyle, 2004). Knowledge of botanical data, such as plant locality, seasonality, and life cycle, can be used to identify controlled substances and noxious weeds. Forensic botany can also help to answer questions surrounding rapes and homicides (Lane et al., 1990). Plants can link suspects to victims and crime scenes, or help to prove or disprove alibis (Ladd and Lee, 2004; Norris and Bock, 2000). The identification of plant cells in the gastrointestinal tract may also be used to trace a victim's last steps, or determine the victim's origin (Bock and Norris, 1991; Bock et al., 1988).

   The determination of PMI is another area in which botanical material can be significant. In particular, plants have been used to determine the

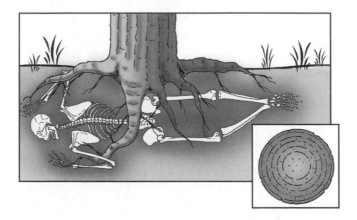

Figure 5.1   Illustration showing how roots grow through skeletal remains. The number of rings in a tree cross-section (shown in inset), can indicate a minimal amount of time that the body has been in a location. For example, this tree, with five rings, indicates that the remains had to have been in this location for a minimum of five years.

length of time a body has been in a specific environment, or if a body has been moved from one location to another. For example, tree roots can be important for law enforcement by providing them with a useful PMI. If the root of a tree is found growing through, around, or into a skeletal element, the root can be useful for determining PMI because roots have growth rings like the rest of the tree, with each ring representing a year. If a root with five rings was found growing into a bone, the PMI would then be five years or more. In other words, the body had to have been in that location for at least five years (Figure 5.1). The PMI would be five years or more because there is no way to know how long the body was buried before the root grew into the skeletal remains. Botanical remains may also be useful for determining whether a body was moved or for tracing the origin of the body, if the botanical remains are not native to the area where the body was recovered.

Forensic palynology, a subdiscipline of forensic botany, uses pollen and spores to help solve crimes (Bryant, 1989; Bryant et al., 1990; Milne et al., 2004). Although the full potential of forensic palynology remains underutilized and ignored in most countries, it can be used to answer a number of questions associated with legal investigations (Horrocks et al., 1998). It is often possible to be very specific about where a person or thing has been from the pollen types that occur together in a sample. Certain plants only occur in particular areas and in certain combinations, so if pollen or spores from particular plants are found together it may indicate geographical origin. Pollen can help destroy or prove alibis, link a suspect to the scene of a crime, or link something left at the crime scene to a suspect (Faegri et al., 1989). It can also help to determine what country or state drugs, food, merchandise, and antiques, among other things, originated. Pollen and spore production and dispersion are important considerations in the study of forensic palynology.

Often, many types of forensic data, such as pollen results, do not actually serve to convict a suspect. Instead, the samples are useful tools that can point investigators in the right direction, or narrow the number of suspects, or perhaps even eliminate a person as a prime suspect. It may also be used as circumstantial evidence in court. Nevertheless, even in this type of supporting role, forensic palynology can become a powerful tool of the forensic investigator.

5.1.1   Collection Procedures for Botanical Evidence

To collect botanical evidence it is important to have the appropriate equipment. A kit for collecting botanical evidence should include, at minimum, the following:

- Rubber gloves
- Root clippers
- Pruning shears
- Tweezers
- Scoops (large spoons)
- Trowels
- Newspaper or paper
- Paper bags
- Plastic containers
- Labels
- Indelible ink pens

Two important points to remember before collecting botanical remains: (1) natural botanical remains can include poison ivy, poison oak, and poison sumac, so do not forget to wear your gloves; and (2) plant remains should never be put into plastic bags, since they may grow mold, they may disintegrate very rapidly, and they can also lose their identifying characteristics. Botanical evidence that is found in body fluid or in mud can be placed in a plastic container, but it must be kept in a cool or cold environment to prevent sample decay. Hall (1988) suggests using a phone book or catalogue to collect samples. The paper is great for absorbing moisture, and allows for drying. Also, newspaper works very well for wrapping samples (Galloway et al., 2001).

After collection, each piece of botanical evidence must be labeled. If you use paper bags or newspaper, information can be written directly on the bag or paper. Each label should contain the following information.

- Case number
- Sample number
- Date and time of collection
- Exact location of sample
- Color, size, and shape of sample
- Name of the collector and any other personnel who handle the sample (to maintain chain of custody)

Botanical samples can include everything from minute samples, such as pollen, to large samples, such as tree roots that have grown through a grave, skeletal remains, clothing, or roots that have been cut to dig a grave. Botanical evidence should be one of the first pieces of evidence collected, even before entomological evidence, to ensure that new botanical evidence is not introduced into the scene by investigators. All vegetation in the area should be photographed, and samples from trees and shrubs should be collected. Any root that is cut for evidence should also be photographed *in situ*, and if any plant material is collected due to growth into clothing or bones, it should also be photographed prior to removal since it may become dislodged during transport or handling. A sample of leaf litter and ground cover should also be collected during the initial sampling.

Next, samples should be collected from the body. Botanical remains on, around, and under the victim should be sampled. If the victim is clothed, Hall (1988) suggests that pant cuffs and pockets are a good place to look for plant material and that all clothing should be examined closely. Here are some of the areas that should be examined carefully for small pieces of botanical evidence:

- Sediment: Soil, dirt, and dust are common elements at almost every crime scene, and they often contain abundant pollen and spores (Pain, 1993). Samples of dirt collected from the clothing, skin, hair, shoes, or car of a victim might prove useful in linking the victim with the location at which the crime occurred (Mildenhall, 1988). The same would be true of any suspects thought to be associated with a crime.
- Hair and cloth: The manufacturing process of woven cloth, woolen blankets, ropes, clothing, and fur ensures that these fabrics all make very effective traps for pollen and spores. Hair, whether human or nonhuman, is also extremely good at trapping pollen and spores.

A summary table for botanical collection procedures is outlined in Table 5.1. If the investigator is unsure of how much material will be needed by the forensic botanist for analysis, the best rule is to collect extra material — as the adage goes, better to be safe than sorry.

Table 5.1 Summary of the Steps Used for the Collection of Botanical Evidence

Prepare collection kit.
Prepare sample labels.
Do not forget to wear gloves to avoid contact with poisonous plants.
Photograph and take samples of all botanical specimens in the crime scene area.
Collect a sample of leaf litter, ground cover, and soil from the site away from the body.
Collect botanical and soil samples around, under, and from the body. If clothing is present, check pant cuffs and pockets for samples. If hair is present, take sample from this area also.
If the body is buried, collect samples from the soil surrounding the body, particularly from areas under the body and soil that is on the body.

5.1.2 How to Find a Forensic Botanist

Finding a forensic botanist is not as easy as finding a forensic anthropologist or entomologist, each of whom have their own recognized board for certification. When choosing a forensic botanist, it is important to choose one that has a Ph.D. and extensive experience in forensic taxonomic identification. At the same time, it is also important to choose a specialist who is familiar with your particular geographic area. Inquiries to law enforcement agencies may lead to recommendations. In addition, since most forensic botanists hold positions in biology departments at universities, one avenue to finding a forensic botanist is to call your local university and inquire. Also, many specialists advertise via Web pages, so a quick search on the Internet may help to find a forensic botanist; however, we recommend further inquiries as to the person's qualifications because anyone can create a Web page.

5.2 Forensic Entomology

The use of entomological evidence in forensic casework is not a recent development. Forensic entomology was first reported to have been used in thirteenth century China (Tz'u, translated by McKnight, 1981) and was used sporadically in the nineteenth century and the early part of the twentieth century (Smith, 1995), playing a part in some major cases. Forensic entomology is the use of insect evidence to answer questions pertaining to legal issues. Entomological evidence can be used to address a variety of issues in a criminal investigation, including: time since death, season of death, geographic location of death, movement or storage of the remains following death, specific sites of trauma on the body, sexual molestation, and the use of drugs (Hall, 1990; Haskell and Catts, 1990; Haskell et al., 1997). However, the principal role of forensic entomology is to address circumstances of death and length of time since death or PMI. According to Haskell et al. (1997), two main approaches exist to determine PMI: (1) determination of the life stages of insects, usually flies, that are associated with the body; and (2) the analysis of the pattern of successive waves of arthropod colonization of a corpse.

Insect colonization of decomposing remains can appear minutes after death and can persist long after a body is skeletonized. The most common insects found in frequency and number of species are from the orders Diptera (flies) and Coleoptera (beetles) (Haskell et al., 1997) as represented in Figure 5.2. The primary role of flies is to feed on carrion (decaying flesh of a corpse). Conversely, the primary role of beetles is one of a predatory nature, feeding on the eggs and larvae of the flies (Haskell et al., 1997), and beetles may also arrive during later stages of body decomposition to feed on dried soft tissue and cartilage (Haskell and Catts, 1990). In addition, it is also important to note that in certain geographical regions, additional insect species may be found in high numbers during specific periods of decomposition.

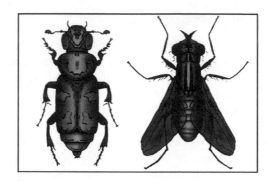

Figure 5.2 This figure shows the morphological differences between a fly (right) and a beetle (left).

5.2.1 *Insect Life Cycle*

The most precise method for establishing PMI is to use a known insect species' life cycle, specifically flies. Laboratory and field studies have generated baseline developmental rates under differing temperature regimes. According to Haskell et al. (1997), precision in generating PMI is fairly good when there are accurate temperature data and species identification.

The generalized life stages of a fly (Figure 5.3) conform to most of the higher species, or evolutionarily advanced flies, which belong to the suborder Cyclorrapha (Castner, 2001; Haskell et al., 1997). Adult female flies generally lay their eggs in close proximity to a food source with moisture, and where

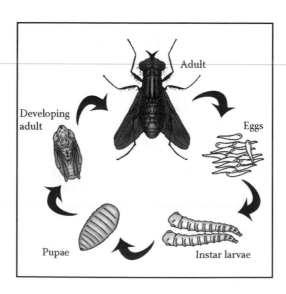

Figure 5.3 Illustration of the life cycle of a fly.

the eggs are protected from direct solar radiation. The most common locations on the body where eggs are deposited include exposed orifices (such as nasal passages, corners of the mouth, and the eyes), open wounds, in folds of clothing close to the face and wounds, in the hair along the ground line, and in sheltered areas formed by the interface of the body with the ground (Haskell and Catts, 1990; Haskell et al., 1997). These areas will decompose faster than other areas because of initial insect colonization. Refer to Haskell et al. (1997), Byrd and Castner (2001a), and Castner (2001) for more detailed descriptions of forensically important insects and the detailed descriptions of the life cycles of flies and beetles.

After fly eggs are laid on a corpse, they will hatch within a few hours giving rise to the first of three growth stages (in-stars) of larvae or maggots (Figure 5.4). The instars are stages of growth during feeding. After the third larval stage, the larvae are finished feeding and migrate away from the remains to burrow into the soil. After this, the larvae will go through a pupal stage, and then hatch into adult flies. During the pupal stage, the outer hardened casing, known as the puparium, develops from the exoskeleton of the third-stage larva. Over time, the puparium shrinks, hardens, and darkens in color from brown, to reddish brown, to almost black. According to Haskell et al. (1997) the color changes are important clues that are used to age puparia. The adult fly emerges after several days of development, leaving behind the empty puparium, and successive fly life cycles continue as the newly hatched female flies lay eggs on the corpse after copulation. The identification and representative collection of all the insect life stages are important for the determination of PMI. Collection of insect larvae and

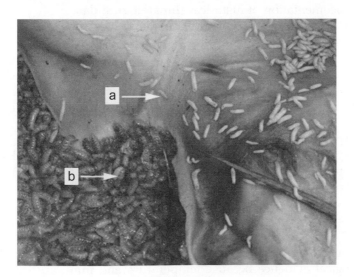

Figure 5.4 Fly larva (maggot) development on a decomposing pig cadaver. The arrows illustrate the different in-star phases of maggot development with the (a) younger larvae; and (b) the older larvae.

puparia will assist in the calculation of the number of insect generations, thus allowing for a more precise determination of PMI.

5.2.2   Collection Procedures for Entomological Evidence

There is considerable diversity in the types of death scene environments such as open wooded areas, burials, vehicles, dumpsters, and enclosed urban structures, such as homes and buildings. The collection of entomological evidence should be a standard procedure at all types of death scenes. A number of published references provide detailed procedural instructions for the collection of entomological evidence (see Byrd and Castner, 2001b; Haskell and Catts, 1990; Haskell et al., 1997; Haskell et al., 2001; Lord and Burger, 1983; Smith, 1995) and should be consulted for further information. The following collection procedures are based upon Haskell et al. (2001).

Haskell et al. (2001) divide the entomological protocols at the death scene into eight steps that are applicable to most geographic areas and habitats:

- Initial observation of insect infestation.
- Initiation of climatological data collection.
- Collection of adult flies and beetles.
- Collection of eggs, larvae, and puparia.
- Collection of specimens from the surrounding area, up to 6 m (19.7 feet), from the body.
- Collection of specimens from directly under and in close proximity to the remains, 1 m or less (3.28 feet or less), after the body has been removed.
- Documentation of historical climatological data.
- Assessment of the ecological characteristics (e.g., soil, plant, water) at the scene.

In addition, Haskell et al. (2001) provides copies of essential data forms that should be completed during the collection process. A few generic sample forms, as well as a collection checklist, are provided in the Appendices section:

- Appendix 2: Entomology Kit Checklist
- Appendix 3: Entomology Notation and Collection Checklist
- Appendix 4: Entomology Specimen Log Sheet
- Appendix 5: Entomology Data Form

5.2.3   Collecting Climatological and Temperature Data

It is essential to have accurate climatological data when estimating PMI from entomological evidence because temperature and humidity largely determine the time required for insects to undergo their life cycle. In addition, it is also suggested that weather data be obtained for a time period from one to two weeks prior to when the death occurred and three to five days past the time the body was discovered (Haskell et al., 2001). Weather data should include hourly temperatures, humidity, extent of cloud cover, precipitation, and wind speed and direction. This information can be obtained by contacting the nearest National Weather Service (NWS) station.

According to Haskell et al. (2001), multiple temperature readings should be taken while processing the death scene:

- Ambient air temperature should be recorded in close proximity to the body at heights of 0.3 and 1.3 m (11.8 in and 4.3 feet).
- The temperature of the ground surface should be recorded by placing the thermometer directly on top of the surface ground cover.
- Body surface temperatures should be recorded by placing the thermometer directly on the body.
- The body ground interface temperature can be obtained by sliding the thermometer between the underside of the body and the ground.
- If observed, maggot mass temperatures are obtained by inserting the thermometer into the center of each mass.
- After the remains are removed, soil temperatures can be obtained by inserting the thermometer directly into the soil where the body was deposited. A second soil temperature should also be obtained 1- to 2-m (3.28 to 6.56 feet) from the body.

5.2.4   Collection of Specimens before Body Removal

5.2.4.1   Collection of Fast Flying and Crawling Insects

The first samples to be collected are the fast flying (flies) and crawling insects (beetles) (Haskell et al., 2001). An aerial net is used for this procedure by sweeping the net rapidly back and forth above the body, or upon vegetation in the area surrounding the body, with a rotation of the net opening 180° after each pass to prevent collected samples from escaping. Another technique that may be utilized is to approach the insects with the tail of the net up with a squatting motion because the natural behavior of the insects is to fly up into the net. After the insects are in the net, the end of the net can be placed into a killing jar that is then capped. The killing jar should contain either gypsum cement (plaster of Paris) or a few cotton balls at the bottom of the jar that are soaked with fresh ethyl acetate. A few minutes in the killing jar should be adequate for immobilization of the insects. The insects can be placed in a dry vial if they are to be processed in a few hours. Otherwise, they can be placed into 75% ethyl alcohol by transferring them into small vials via a small funnel. Furthermore, any ground-crawling adults can be collected with forceps or fingers and should be preserved in the same manner as the flying adults.

5.2.4.2   Collection of Insects on the Body

After the area over the body and the surrounding area have been processed, insects can be collected from the body before it is removed. Extreme caution

```
┌──────────────────────────────────────────────────────────┐
│                                                          │
│   Case and Time:                                         │
│   Case #:                                                │
│   Location:                                              │
│   Sample #:                                              │
│                                                          │
└──────────────────────────────────────────────────────────┘
```

Figure 5.5   Sample label. (Adapted from Haskell et al., 2001.)

should be taken when removing entomological material from the body so no inadvertent postmortem artifacts are left and no evidence is disturbed.

A sample containing eggs and a mixed sample of larval stages (several hundred) should be collected and preserved by placing the sample in a vial with one of the specified preservatives (see Appendix 6). A label, filled out with pencil and not ink, must be included with each sample. Each label should include the sample number, time, date, case number, and city or county (see Figure 5.5). In addition, double labels should be a standard practice; an external label should be adhered to the vial and an internal label should be placed within the vial with the specimens. Double labels ensure that if the outside label comes off, then the pertinent information will still be located in the vial.

A second live sample should also be collected because living samples can be reared to adults in the laboratory to confirm larval identification (Haskell et al., 2001). A second equal-sized portion of maggots should be placed into specialized maggot-rearing cups that will keep the specimens alive during shipment to an entomologist. A piece of aluminum foil (15 cm × 18 cm, or 6 in × 7 in) can be used to easily construct larval rearing pouches by folding it into thirds horizontally, then again into thirds vertically. The end product piece is a small rectangle (5 cm × 7 cm, or 2 in × 3 in) that can be unfolded into an open-topped three-dimensional rectangular pouch by crimping together the corners. A small piece of beef liver (90 to 150 g, or 3 oz to 5 oz) is added to the pouch as a food source to keep 30 to 60 maggots alive during shipment. The pouch should be crimped to seal the maggots inside and then placed in a vented, pint-sized (0.5 liters or 16 oz) cardboard or plastic container with approximately 2.5 cm (approximately 1 in) of medium-sized vermiculite or sand in the bottom.

Eggs are packaged in the same manner as the maggots, but the puparia can be placed directly into the shipping containers that have vermiculite or sand, without the tinfoil pouch and liver. A food source is not needed because the puparia do not feed. However, beetle larvae, generally recognized as having three pairs of legs (Figure 5.6), should also be collected, but not added to the live fly maggots. Many beetle larvae are predacious on fly larvae and should be packaged separately. A food source such as beef liver or fly maggots should be added to the package.

Figure 5.6 Fly larva (left) and beetle larva (right) are different in many ways. In particular, beetle larvae have pairs of legs while the fly larvae have no legs.

5.2.4.3 Collection of Insects That Have Migrated from the Body

The investigator should also focus on collecting insects that have completed feeding and migrated away from the body because these insects will be older than those found on the remains. Collection of these samples can be found within a 6 m (approximately 20 feet) radius depending on the terrain. See the following section for detailed instructions for collecting insect material within the organic debris on the surface and the soil.

5.2.5 Collection of Specimens after Body Removal

In instances of bodies recovered from outdoor settings, there may be a considerable number of entomological specimens still left on the ground surface, hidden in organic material, or burrowed in the soil (Haskell et al., 2001). Specimens from each immature stage should be collected and a second sample should be collected alive for rearing. Samples of litter and other organic materials should also be collected down to the soil for hidden insects and placed in cardboard or plastic containers (suggested size: 2-quarts or 1.9-liters) for examination in the laboratory. In addition, approximately six soil samples that average 10 cm^3 in size (4 in^3) should also be collected directly under the location of the body and up to 1-m (3-feet) from the body. This material can be sifted and screened at the recovery site, or placed into cardboard or plastic containers for examination in the laboratory.

Table 5.2 Summary of the Steps Taken to Collect Entomological Evidence

1. Prepare collection kit
2. Prepare labels
3. Observe scene for the presence of insects
4. Collect climate and ecological data from scene (during the time of recovery and a week after):
   a. Record ambient air temperature close to the body
   b. Record temperature of ground surface
   c. Record body surface temperature
   d. Record body-ground interface temperature
   e. Record maggot mass temperatures
   f. Record soil temperatures after body removal
5. Collect insects from area around the body (up to 6 m):
   a. Collect adult flies and beetles (flying and crawling insects)
   b. Collect eggs, larvae, and puparia (on the body and those that have crawled away)
6. Collect insects from directly under and around remains, 1 m or less, after the body has been removed
7. Collect historical climate data 2 weeks prior to the discovery of the body from the National Weather Service

Source: Adapted from   Haskell et al., 2001.

As previously mentioned with the collection of botanical evidence, if the investigator is unsure of how much entomological evidence is needed for future analysis, collect extra if possible. A summary of entomological collection procedures is outlined in Table 5.2.

5.2.6   How to Find a Forensic Entomologist

If it is not possible to have a forensic entomologist present during the recovery of a body, it may be necessary to find one to analyze the material collected from a scene. When choosing a forensic entomologist, it is important to choose one that has a Ph.D. and extensive experience in taxonomic identification of forensic-related insect and arthropod species. At the same time, it is also important to choose a specialist that is familiar with your particular geographic area of the country. They should be active academically and have membership in the American Academy of Forensic Sciences, membership in the Entomological Society of America, and they should be board certified by the American Board of Forensic Entomology (ABFE). Currently there are only seven board-certified forensic entomologists in North America. These individuals can be located by logging on to the official website of the ABFE (www.missouri.edu/~agwww/entomology/index.html). A list of the Diplomats is provided on this Web site, with the necessary contact information.

chapter 6

Survey and Mapping Techniques

Searching for, recovering, and collecting evidence from a burial or surface scatter are disruptive processes that occur during a forensic investigation. Once something is removed, it can never be put back in its exact place. Survey and mapping techniques allow investigators to maintain a record of where every item of evidence was found within a defined area, and if necessary, will allow the investigator to recreate the order of events that took place concerning these items.

Surveying and mapping are skills that many incorrectly believe to be beyond their ability, yet a clear review of the techniques involved and a little practice in the field can turn the beginner into a specialist very quickly. In fact, without such basic surveying and mapping skills, no forensic investigator should venture into the serious business of site destruction, known to forensic archaeologists as excavation. This chapter aims to help forensic investigators achieve a respectable level of mapping skills with a minimum of technical explanation.

6.1 Scales for Recording Data

The end result of all surveying and mapping is to make a plan, or view from above, of what was in evidence on the site. This means that what is drawn on paper will have to be many times smaller than reality—in other words, scaled to size. The ratio of real size to drawn size will depend upon the particular reality that it is necessary to depict, the size of the paper available, and the purpose of the plan.

It is important to consider the question of scale prior to recording any information, since this is one of the factors that will determine how accurately the measurements should be read. Metric unit scales are recommended for forensic investigation due to the ease of converting measurements to the chosen scale and grids available on preprinted graph paper. For this reason, all measurements in this chapter are given in metric units. Please refer to

Appendix 7 for metric to standard measurement conversion information. A ratio of 1:10 (1 cm on paper = 10 cm measurement) is the standard for most burials, areas of concentrated evidence, and any other detailed relations of evidence. Drawings of widely scattered evidence are typically recorded in a ratio of 1:100 (1 cm on paper = 100 cm or 1 m measurement) and usually consist of labeled points within the full limits of the site. It is also a good practice to adopt a standard size of graph paper (for example, 8.5 × 11 in letter, 11 × 17 in tabloid) with five squares per block grid as, over time, this creates a familiarity with scale when recording data.

6.2 Accuracy in Recording Data

It is important to maintain a sense of neatness and accuracy in maps and corresponding field notes. Notes should be clear, legible, and understandable not only to the person recording the data but to other people. Messy maps, bad field notes, and the processes of copying into neater formats typically generate errors that can be easily avoided. Always check your work, and whenever possible, do it by a different method than the one used the first time. Elaborate checks are usually not necessary and checks can be something as simple as sight alignments to see if things are in certain relative positions.

Also, there is no point in taking the time and trouble to measure something to exceptional accuracy if it is impossible to plot the work onto paper with a corresponding degree of accuracy. For example, it might be possible to measure the width of a burial feature to the nearest millimeter, but on a 1:10 or 1:100 scaled map, one millimeter will not be discernable. Always be sure that your measurements are reflective of what can actually be recorded with accuracy.

6.3 Transit Survey Systems

In using transit survey systems for mapping, the instrument operator records the horizontal angle, elevation, and distance between a known reference point and a desired survey point. Reduced to the basics, a transit is a telescope mounted on a horizontal circular protractor. Inside the telescope are vertical and horizontal target cross hairs. This assembly rotates horizontally in reference to a circular lower plate scaled from 0° to 360°, also known as vernier readings. The transit assembly is mounted onto a tripod and is always leveled before obtaining vertical and horizontal measurements.

When a transit is used in combination with a stadia rod, which is marked with known measures, distances can be measured along with horizontal angles and elevations. Stadia distance is based on two fine stadia cross hairs that are mounted horizontally inside the telescope, so when the operator looks through the telescope, the wires are optically superimposed on the stadia rod marks (Figure 6.1). The operator observes the amount of stadia rod visible between the cross hairs and can equate that to a distance from the transit to the stadia

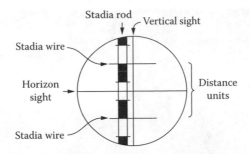

Figure 6.1 Example of cross hairs seen through the transit telescope superimposed onto the stadia rod.

rod, as well as determine any elevation changes between the transit point and the base of the stadia rod (Figure 6.2). The vernier reading from the transit to the stadia rod marks any changes in horizontal angles.

Most mechanical transits have been replaced by electronic distance measuring instruments (EDMIs), sometimes referred to as total stations (Figure 6.3). The total station transit is a computerized unit capable of calculating and holding data generated during a survey. The total station transits emit a laser signal directed toward a stadia prism that reflects the signal back to the transit. The unit then calculates the horizontal angle of reflection, vertical angle changes, and any other programmed functions from the transit's position in relation to the stadia prism. The data are later downloaded into a computer software application for analysis and plotting a map. The software used in this type of unit typically allows the operator to type in a text identifier for each point as it is measured. Total station transits have become increasingly popular in forensic investigations, as they are a very efficient means of mapping forensic scenes, allow for greater detail and accuracy in measurement, and the data can be analyzed in various ways depending on the software applications being used.

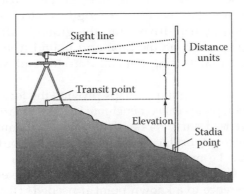

Figure 6.2 Measuring distance and elevation using a transit and stadia rod.

Figure 6.3   Orange County Crime Scene investigator Ronnie Murdock using a total station transit. (Photo courtesy of J. Mulligan.)

6.3.1   Datum Points and Benchmarks

A major control point is needed when mapping any burial area to maintain consistency in all measurements. A datum is a fixed point of reference for all depth and angle measurements made during the recovery of remains. The datum needs to be permanent since all measurements within the boundaries of the burial site are taken from this point, and it may serve as the reference point for any future work at the site as well. Trees, fence posts, and other seemingly permanent features should not be used as a datum due to their ease of removal. Building corners, utility poles, or datum points that you have added to the scene tend to be the most permanent and reliable points for use. For example, a length of steel rod or pipe is an excellent datum point when driven into the ground. After use, mark the surface level of the ground on the pipe and pound it into the ground. It can easily be located later using a metal detector and reset to its proper height.

USGS (U.S. Geological Survey) maps provide the locations of precisely determined elevation points called benchmarks. These marks are established in the field by licensed surveyors and are made of stamped brass disks affixed to rock outcrops, bridges, buildings, or other prominent features. Multiple points can be measured along a distance from a benchmark to obtain an accurate elevation for a datum or to record the exact location of a burial scene in reference to a known point if needed. This is referred to as tying in your datum to the official USGS elevations.

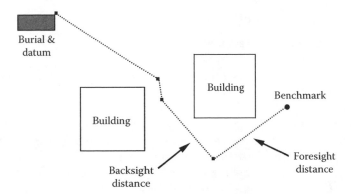

Figure 6.4 Measuring distance between the benchmark and survey points and around objects.

To tie your burial scene datum in to a benchmark, you may have to work around obstructions or measure long distances using a method of leapfrogging from one point to another with a transit and stadia rod or a total station. This is done through a series of foresighting, measuring from a known point to an unknown point, and backsighting, measuring from an unknown point to a known point. This method gives accurate distances and angles from a fixed or known point to your datum through a series of established points (Figure 6.4):

- Determine a starting mark on a benchmark or other known elevation.
- Set a foresight measurement from the starting point to a distant point marked with the stadia rod.
- Record the horizontal angle and elevation from the transit to the distant point.
- Mark the newly recorded point with a stake and then move the transit to a point beyond this new point.
- Once the transit is set and leveled at its new location, take a backsight measurement to the stadia rod being held at the previously marked point.
- Record the horizontal angle and elevation from the stadia rod to the transit.
- Once the backsight point has been recorded, the stadia rod is then moved to a point distant from the transit and the process is repeated until the datum within the burial scene is tied in.

If a total station is used in the field, it is highly recommended that the information be recorded in the field notes as a backup just in case any problems later occur during the downloading of data. The total station is, however, considered to be the primary data source if any conflicts occur between the written and electronic records.

6.4   Compass Survey

If survey equipment is not available, compass surveying will also allow you to obtain a degree bearing from north (0°/360°) of an object or line from an established or known point. A field compass used in conjunction with a 50-meter field tape can provide angle and distance measurements that can be used at a later date to relocate a datum from a known point. This information is especially helpful when working in an area where the terrain has heavy ground cover or in cases where the use of flagging tape may draw unwanted attention to the area of investigation.

The simplest type of field compass usually consists of a compass dial supported by a handheld base-plate with index or directional markings. This type of compass is typically used for orienteering on a map during outdoor activities such as hiking, but can also be used for simple mapping if a more accurate compass is not available. The preferred type of field compass for forensic mapping is a prismatic or pocket transit compass (Figure 6.5). These compasses have some sort of forward sighting mark, often incorporated into a hinged lid. The rear sight usually swings up into position or is marked on a base-plate and lines up with the forward sight. The user lines up both sights with the target object and the prism or mirror then reflects the compass dial so the bearing to the object can be read. The user may also line up the sights on a specific sightline so a distant object can be placed in relation to the point of origin, such as the placement of a corner stake or a baseline used in mapping. Some of the more expensive prismatic or pocket transit compasses are also designed for survey purposes and can be mounted onto a leveling staff for elevation and distance measurement. When taking line bearings, the prismatic compass is held in the hand or supported by a leveling staff and is accurate to about half a degree.

Figure 6.5   Example of a prismatic compass with a forward sight mirrored lid and base-plate with a rear sight.

To determine angle and distance measurements using the compass survey method:

- Determine a starting mark on a benchmark or other known point.
- Run a meter tape from the starting point to a distant point and record the distance measurement.
- From the starting point, align the index or center line of your base-plate compass or the forward and rear sights of the prismatic compass over the tape line.
- Holding the base-plate or prismatic compass firmly in hand, rotate the compass dial until the magnetic needle and the N or 0°/360° on the vernier dial are aligned.
- Read the bearing of the index line on the base-plate compass or the reflected dial on the prismatic mirror (still aligned with the tape line) as it passes through the vernier dial and record the degree of angle to the distant point.
- Once the bearing for the distant point is recorded, mark the point with a stake.
- Follow the same procedure in backsighting and foresighting as described above in transit surveying until the datum point is reached.

When using a compass, precautions should be taken against local interference from magnetic materials, such as steel and iron objects.

6.5 Selecting a Framework for Mapping

When first faced with the responsibility of surveying or mapping an area, most beginners are at a loss as to how to start. The secret is to mark the site limits, choose a framework for recording the evidence, and then relate the details to the framework. The surveying and mapping of a forensic site involves two basic frameworks for recording the evidence. The first framework, a control-point map, is concerned with finding the position of objects in relation to a known point. The second, a grid-system map, is concerned with laying out grid squares to mark limits within the burial site, control the work area, and record evidence in great detail.

In control-point mapping, investigators locate the evidence and make the best possible record of it. This framework typically involves survey equipment or simple mapping tools when evidence is spaced out across a larger area, such as surface scatters or in areas surrounding the burial. In grid-system mapping, there is a certain element of choice in methods and investigators must decide what is within the limitations of the investigation. This framework is usually best applied over a burial or concentrated areas of evidence scatter as the detail of positioning is much more precise. However, the same basic principles are used in whichever approach is taken.

These frameworks are directed toward putting a plan or diagram on paper as an accurate representation of what was found or what was done at the site. To create acceptable site and burial maps, at least three kinds of information should be derived from a known point for each piece of evidence: direction, horizontal distance, and vertical distance. This information is easily obtainable by following the techniques discussed here.

6.5.1   Setting Limits and Datum for Mapping

The first concern in either framework is marking the limits of the area to be mapped. Using wooden corner stakes and either flagging tape or survey string to mark the limits, a rectangle is typically constructed to designate the area to be mapped. It is best to start your limits well outside of the area containing any evidence. This ensures that everything will be easily included in your map for later analysis. If possible, it is also recommended that you orient your marked area in either a north-south or east-west direction to simplify measuring angles when mapping. Always be consistent by using metric units throughout your mapping and recovery stages.

To construct the limits around the evidence, a 3-4-5 triangle is used in the following manner (Figure 6.6):

- Set the first corner stake.
- Using a compass, establish a north-south or east-west line extending from this stake. This is referred to as setting a baseline (Figure 6.7).
- Along the baseline orientation, set a stake on a measurement that is a multiple of four (i.e., 4, 8, 12, 16) and lies outside of the area containing evidence.

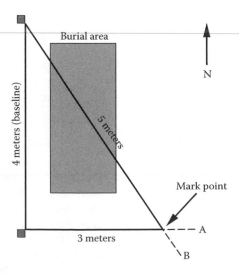

Figure 6.6   Setting up a 3-4-5 triangle from the baseline for a rectangle.

Figure 6.7 Author Sandra Wheeler assists a student in setting up a baseline using a compass and tape measure.

- Secure a meter tape (tape A) to the first corner stake and at a right angle to the newly established baseline, run the tape out to a distance equivalent to a multiple of three (i.e., 3, 6, 9, 12).
- Secure an additional tape (tape B) to the post at the opposite end of the baseline and run it out at an angle toward the endpoint of tape A.
- Holding one tape in your right hand and the other in your left hand, bring them together as level as possible; assuming that the baseline is 4-m long, tape A and tape B should cross at the 3 and 5 m marks respectively, forming a 3-4-5 triangle; mark this crossing point as your third corner point (a hypotenuse table is provided in Appendix 8 for measurements outside of the basic 3-4-5 multiples) (Figure 6.8).
- Repeat the angle measurement from the baseline to mark your final corner point.
- Using a compass and measuring tape, check for right angles and equal lengths on opposite sides of your rectangle.

Now that the mapping limits have been set, a datum can be established to aid in recording the contours of the ground surface and measuring the depth of any evidence recovered from below the ground surface. The datum is very important and careful thought should be given in setting this point. The datum should be in a position that is clear of all obstructions in relation to the evidence being mapped and be positioned above any elevation changes in the ground surface. In many cases, one of the corner stakes set

Figure 6.8   Author Sandra Wheeler assists students in setting up the boundaries of a 3-4-5 grid.

along the baseline of the area limit can serve as a datum point; however, a separate point or post is highly recommended. To use the datum point to measure elevations and depths (Figure 6.9):

- Tie a length of survey string equivalent to the area length around the top of the datum (if using a wooden stake, use a nail in the end of the stake, or if using a metal rod or pipe, use a piece of electrical tape to secure the position of the string).
- Mark the ground surface onto the datum and record the height above ground for the survey string, commonly referred to as a datum line.
- Attach a line level to the datum line and extend it out over the surface contour or object to be measured.

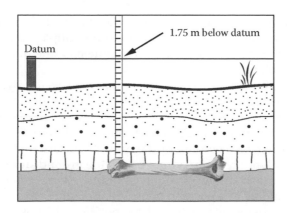

Figure 6.9   Example of measuring the depth of objects below the datum.

- Keeping the datum line level, set the initial end of a stick tape on the point to be measured and adjust so that the stick tape is at a right angle to the datum line.
- Read the height of the datum line where it crosses the stick tape and record the depth of the contour or object below the datum.
- Repeat this process for any contour or object that is of forensic interest throughout the mapping and recovery stages.

If objects are located at a depth of more than 1 m, it is suggested that you carefully use a plumb bob along with the stick tape to maintain a right angle for the measurements.

6.5.2 Control-Point Mapping

When a skeleton is deposited on the ground surface, there are a number of ways to map the scattered remains depending on the degree of dispersal. When evidence is spaced out across a larger area, such as surface scatters or additional areas of interest around a burial, control-point mapping is the most efficient framework for recording data. Area limits can be quite extensive in some cases and large sections of ground surface can be mapped quickly using measurements taken at a right angle from the baseline of the established limits. To use the control-point framework:

- Determine the limits of the scatter.
- Establish a baseline either to one side of the scatter or down the middle of the scatter depending on how dispersed the remains are.
- Beginning at the corner closest to the zero mark along the baseline, use an additional tape to measure the distance from the baseline to any object being mapped, maintaining a 90° angle between the baseline and your distance tape by using a compass or right angle tool (Figure 6.10).

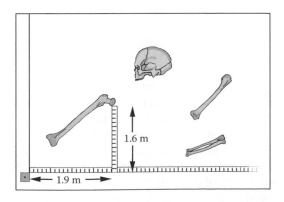

Figure 6.10 Example of measuring objects using control-point method of mapping.

- Take the distance reading along the baseline tape and then from the second tape out to the object being mapped; also record the depth of the object relative to the datum.
- Proceed across the area limits recording the position of evidence in relation to the baseline and the datum for each item encountered.

To create the plan drawing of the area:

- On graph paper, lay out the area limits to scale (1:10 or 1:100) and mark the scaled location of the baseline within the area.
- Record each item's location to scale on the plan drawing in relation to the baseline; record the item's description, measured location, and depth in your field notes.

Control-point mapping can also be conducted using a transit or total station. The advantage of using a total station is that you do not have to establish a baseline. Depending on the size and geography of the site, the total station may be used to map the whole site from one position because it can rotate 360°. To produce a plan using survey equipment:

- Set the datum as described above.
- Set up the transit over this point.
- Mark each object to be recorded with the base of the stadia rod and take a foresight reading of the distance and angle from the transit to the stadia rod.
- Also record the distance, horizontal angle and vertical angle readings in your field notes.

When using a transit for control-point mapping, a plan drawing must be created using a protractor and an engineer's scale to accurately record the positions of mapped objects to scale. If a total station is used, the data can be downloaded into an appropriate software application to create the plan drawing. Examples of plan view maps produced by a total station are presented in Figures 6.11 and Figure 6.12.

6.5.3   Grid-System Mapping

Grid-system mapping of a burial or concentrated areas of evidence scatter are much more time consuming in relation to control-point mapping; nevertheless, this framework allows for a much more detailed recording of the location of each item found within a specific area. In most cases, a 3 m × 4 m rectangle should be large enough to accommodate a burial feature and allow for a closed-security area in which to work within a larger site limit. This method also allows for better control over the work area as specific regions within the grid can be mapped with even more detailed accuracy. When setting up the work area, extreme caution should be taken to not destroy or move

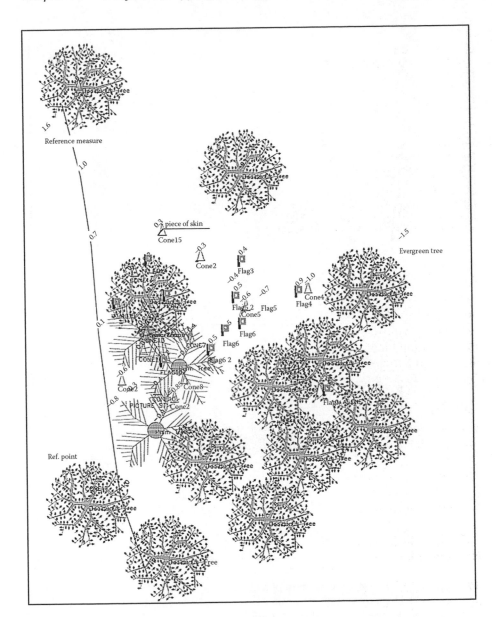

Figure 6.11   Crime scene plan map of a surface scatter produced by a total station transit showing evidence markers and large trees that were within the crime scene. (Courtesy of Orange County Sheriff's Office, Florida.)

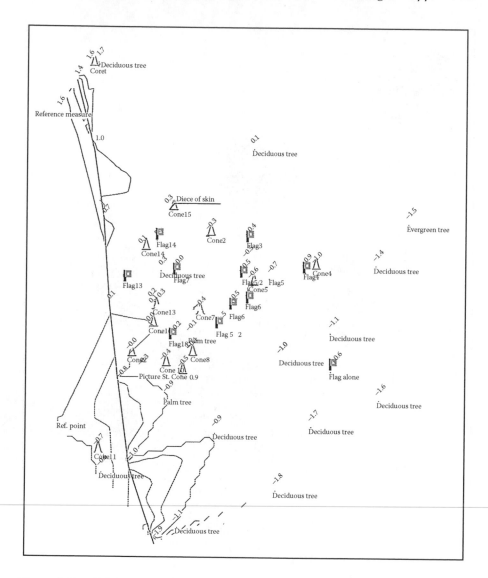

Figure 6.12 Crime scene plan map of a surface scatter (the same map as in Figure 6.11) produced by a total station transit showing evidence markers and contour lines. (Courtesy of Orange County Sheriff's Office, Florida.)

any evidence. Be sure that all photographs and notes have been completed for the area before setting up the limits for a grid system. To work within this framework:

- Establish a rectangular limit around the area using the 3-4-5 method and set the datum as described above.
- Along the sides and ends of the rectangle, set a stake at every 1 m interval.

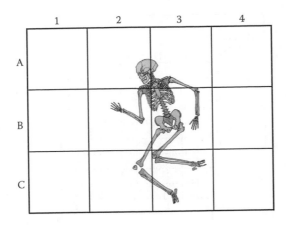

Figure 6.13 Example of a grid placed over a burial area and used for marking horizontal and vertical locations of an object.

- Tie survey string across the rectangle from each stake to its opposite, forming a pattern of 1 m grid-squares; grid strings should be laid out far enough off the surface of the ground so they do not interfere with any surface features or remains.
- Label the baseline grid-squares with numbers and the end squares with letters to identify each square meter (Figure 6.13).

To create the plan drawing of the area:

- On graph paper, lay out the rectangle to scale (1:10 is recommended) and label the grid squares in the same order as above.
- When evidence is encountered, use a measuring tape and stick tape to obtain the precise location of the object or contour within its associated grid square using the grid identifier and horizontal measurements; record the item description and depth in your field notes and the determined position within its scaled grid-square on the plan drawing.

In some instances, it may be helpful to have two or more measurements for different points on certain objects, such as both ends of a long bone, to show the orientation of the object. Heavily localized remains can also be recorded in more detail by using a frame grid that can overlay a 1-m area. Frame grids are typically a 1-m square that has been subdivided into 10-cm squares by wires or strings attached to the frame. These subsquares are then labeled with a letter and number identifier that can place an object within its exact location on the full grid (see Figure 6.14). For example, if you have a collection of items being mapped with a grid frame, a location may be noted as "Grid B6/D3/21cm." This means that the item was found in the meter grid square B6 and within that square it is located in the 10-cm subsquare D3. The "21cm" is a notation of how far below the datum the object rests.

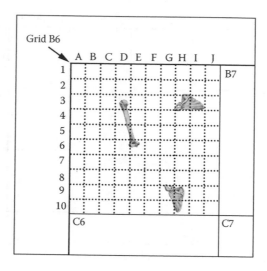

Figure 6.14   Using a frame grid placed over localized remains for detailed mapping.

6.5.4   *Sectional Drawings from Mapped Data*

Sectional drawings are used to depict depth relations between objects. A very simplistic way of viewing a sectional drawing is to consider it as being a vertical slice through the area being mapped. These drawings can be easily created from the depth measurements taken from the datum for each object and for surface contours, additional feature evidence, and soil layers. To create a sectional drawing (Figure 6.15):

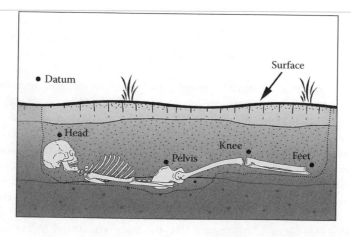

Figure 6.15   Example of a cross-section drawing using depth measurements taken during excavation. This portrays the relative position of the body within the grave.

- On graph paper, mark a point to represent the datum.
- From the datum point, mark the depth of any surface contours; connect the points of these surface contours to create a horizon line.
- Below the horizon line, mark the depths of all mapped objects and soil layers; be sure to label each point and layer as it is marked to avoid any confusion.

6.5.5 Mapping on a Slope

All of the above techniques assume that your site is a flat or gently sloping one. However, in practice, forensic investigators are likely to come up against ravines, rock falls, forested hollows, and human-constructed embankments that will call for a certain amount of ingenuity. When measuring on steep slopes, the most important thing to remember is to be very cautious when moving across the slope and to keep the measuring tapes horizontal through the use of intermediate points in reference to the datum. A traditional transit or total station can also be used in this process; however, this approach usually requires someone with extensive knowledge of the equipment to maintain the accuracy of the measurements.

The control-point framework is used to record evidence located on a steep slope:

- Establish a baseline across the top of the slope where the evidence is located.
- Form a 3-4-5 rectangle off of the ends of the baseline using 3 m and 5 m lengths of survey string with line levels to identify the next two corner points.
- Record the locations of any evidence and surface contours using one of the upper corners as a datum and the control-point mapping framework described earlier; always use a line level when taking measurements from the baseline and datum while working on a slope.
- Establish a new 3-4-5 rectangle that will lie below the previous one in a stairstep formation; use the lower corner points from the initial rectangle as a baseline for the new one (Figure 6.16).
- Use one of the upper corners of the new rectangle as an intermediate datum; measure the height differential between the initial datum and the newer intermediate datum and add this height differential to all depth measurements taken within the new area.
- Repeat this process moving down the slope until all evidence has been recorded.

In addition to a control-point plan map, a section drawing of the slope can also be scaled onto graph paper using the recorded depth measurements to provide details of the distribution of evidence down the slope (Figure 6.17).

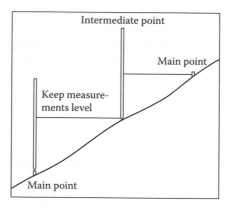

Figure 6.16   Example of using intermediate datum points when recovering or mapping remains found on a slope.

6.5.6   *Records of Recovery*

The combination of a sectional drawing and a plan drawing may later prove to be the most important records of the scene of recovery, so extreme care should be taken when recording the depths and relative positions of evidence in relation to any layers of material that are encountered during recovery. For instance, authors Wheeler and Williams were involved in the search for and recovery of a missing individual who had been beaten to death and buried in a preexisting hole in the cement floor of a barn. The hole had been dug earlier in the year to install a water pump, however, the pump was never installed and the cement floor was never repaired. This made a very convenient location for the quick disposal of a body.

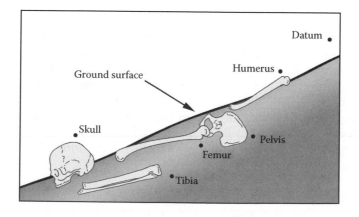

Figure 6.17   A section drawing depicting the locations of scattered remains on a slope. Depths were measured from intermediate datum points along the slope.

After initial investigation, evidence pointed to the hole in the cement floor as the place of burial. The hole was excavated as if it had been a burial in an outdoor setting and detailed control-point mapping was used due to the confined work area. A datum was established and all objects, surface contours and layers that were encountered were mapped and recorded with depths and descriptions. Fragments of the cement pad and the soil under the flooring, removed for the installation of the water pump, were used as backfill over the body. The locations of the fragments were mapped on the plan drawing as they were exposed and the top and bottom depths of each fragment were also noted on a section drawing.

When the body of the missing individual was encountered, it was evident that the victim was much larger than the size of the water pump, which was originally to be placed in the hole. During burial, the cement pad had been undercut to remove additional soil and enlarge the area under the floor to accommodate the victim's body. The head of the victim, positioned in this undercut, was carefully mapped on the plan and sectional drawings prior to the removal of the body. No other debris or fragments of cement were found in the undercut.

Upon review of the case by the Coroner's Office, it was necessary to eliminate the possibility that the fractures to the victim's skull had been caused by dropping the cement fragments into the hole during burial rather than the fractures being sustained during beating at the time of death. When the plan and sectional drawings were consulted, it was evident that the victim's head was covered with a soil layer and was located approximately 15 cm below the depth of the nearest cement fragment. Moreover, it was also evident that any material used to backfill the hole during burial could not have dropped directly onto the victim's head, causing the fractures to the skull, as it was positioned under the existing cement floor in the undercut area. The accuracy of the plan and sectional drawings in this case allowed the coroner to eliminate any possibility of additional damage to the victim's skull during the process of burial and attribute all of the fractures to injuries sustained during the last moments of the individual's life.

6.6 Global Positioning Systems

A Global Positioning System (GPS) can be a valuable mapping tool for recording site locations, delineating site boundaries, and recording the position of skeletal material or evidence within a site. GPS site coordinates can also be used to relocate sites that were recorded in the past. A GPS is made up of a linked system of approximately 24 satellites developed by the U.S. military for global navigation. The system permits electronic receivers to determine exact positions 24 hours a day, any place on Earth, in any weather conditions. GPS receivers obtain signals from four or more satellites simultaneously to calculate the user's position based on time differences in signal uplink and download. One major advantage of using GPS coordinates for mapping is that the data can be downloaded and used in Global Information Systems (GIS) software that integrates your coordinates into preexisting maps.

Absolute GPS accuracy was subject to the U.S. Department of Defense Selective Availability Policy until February 2000. This policy required GPS data to be randomly degraded so that the signal uplink and download codes made available to the general public were only 95% accurate or within 16 m to 100 m of the actual ground position (Van Sickle, 2004). Currently, field-pack submeter units, accurate within 1 m to 5 m, are available commercially but are much more expensive than the typical handheld units used in outdoor activities and small-scale mapping. Most handheld units still have a wide range of variability (3 m to 15 m) but are much more accurate than those used prior to the February 2000 policy change. GPS error rates overall are variable from unit to unit and it is recommended that readings be confirmed by an alternate mapping method or a total station if GPS units are used in forensic investigation.

6.7   *Photograph and Map Resources*

Aerial photographs are an excellent resource for any area being searched. The photographs typically show details of the types of terrain to be covered and any obstructions or urban development in the area. Comparison of older photographs with ones that are more current can also aid in determining how much of the terrain has changed over time. Aerial photographs are readily available for most of the United States and Canada through a variety of sources:

- U.S. Geological Survey (USGS)
- U.S. Soil Conservation Service
- U.S. Forest Service
- Bureau of Land Management
- County planning commissions
- Local and government civil engineering agencies
- Local and government water management agencies
- TerraServer

The photographs are usually representative of standard scale measurements used in public works construction and geological mapping projects. For example, USGS aerial photographs are typically in a 1:6000 scale covering areas of approximately 3 square miles.

Topographic maps supply information not found on standard road atlas maps. These maps provide accurate details of terrain, vegetation patterns, streams, roads, soil types, and many other natural and human-made features. The most widely used topographic maps are from the USGS 7.5 minute series, which is complete for all of the U.S. except for Alaska. This series is printed in a 1:24,000 scale covering an area of approximately 50 square miles.

Many maps and aerial photographs are readily available from agency Web sites and are downloadable free of charge. Many of the images are generic EPS files and can be printed on PC or Macintosh platforms. A few of the agencies with this type of service include the USGS, the U.S. Environmental Protection Agency (EPA), and the Land Boundary Information Systems (LABIS). The maps and photographs available from the EPA are exceptionally helpful when lakes, rivers, canals and shorelines are areas of primary focus in a forensic search. LABIS is an excellent source for detailed county area, railroad, side road, or logging area maps.

chapter 7

The Application of Forensic Archaeology to Crime Scene Investigations

Historically, the analytical expertise of forensic investigators and archaeologists has been combined on numerous occasions. Both fields of research emerged during the nineteenth century, and both disciplines were concerned with the proper identification of materials encountered during investigation (Davis, 1992; Renfrew and Bahn, 2000). There is a theme common to the work of archaeologists and the work of forensic investigators; both attempt to understand the nature, sequence, and underlying reasons for certain events in the past. Their final goals may differ, but their philosophy is much the same. Both disciplines use and present evidence in order to prove their cases.

Most forensic investigators will rarely supervise the recovery of buried remains and are generally not prepared to process this type of scene. Many times the common tactic is to recover the remains as quickly as possible, which can lead to the destruction of valuable evidence and easily damage skeletal material. Most experienced archaeologists will have excavated numerous human remains during their careers, under different conditions and in different soil environments. Archaeologists have been taught how to locate, excavate, and record a human skeleton in order to maximize the information that may help in determining its date, the manner of its deposition, or the relationship of any associated objects or surviving elements such as clothing — all before it is removed from the ground. An archaeologist who has worked in a forensic setting has the added benefit of fully understanding crime scene protocols and the evidentiary requirements of others involved in the scene.

The application of archaeological techniques to crime scene excavation can greatly assist the investigator in accurately and thoroughly recording and recovering all potential evidence, aid in exactly reconstructing and documenting the entire scene, and in answering questions as to the individual's identity and what happened to them, and if applicable, help determine who perpetrated the crime.

Clyde Snow, a noted forensic anthropologist, has stated, "…systematic recovery of the materials from burial and surface sites is best accomplished by suitably modifying methods long employed by archaeologists to solve similar problems" (1982: 118). The purpose of this chapter is to introduce terminology and describe basic archaeological techniques that would provide the most effective and efficient excavation and recovery methods when utilized at forensic scenes.

Archaeology and forensic investigation are both based on highly detailed modes of data collection, documentation, data processing, and analysis. Successful investigations in both fields are similarly oriented in reconstructing what happened at the scene based on physical evidence. In terms of contemporary evidence gathering, it could be said that archaeologists work on some of the coldest cases in existence. It is understood that "each [type of investigation] gathers data in the hope of reconstructing events in order to solve a problem. Each looks for the agents responsible for the physical evidence. Each should operate through the cooperation of many disciplines working together to provide a complete response to the available data" (Davis, 1992: 152). If the investigative techniques are common, this is in part due to the fact that, in both cases, artifacts are the major source of evidence. In archaeology, artifactual evidence is used to understand the behavior of human populations and their relationships with one another and their environment. In forensic investigation, artifactual evidence is used to reconstruct events or to relate an object or a person from one place to another.

Forensic archaeology involves the use of standard archaeological principles and methods to locate and recover human remains and associated evidence within the context of a forensic investigation. The chief concern of both the forensic archaeologist and the crime scene investigator is the legal acquisition of evidence that will be used to establish connections between suspect, victim, and crime, as well as the potential use in future legal proceedings. By using methods familiar to both parties, shared resources and cooperation can lead to more effective and efficient results. When working with a forensic archaeologist, an investigator may be able to take advantage of (Dirkmaat and Adovasio, 1997; Morse et al., 1983):

- Using a systematic and controlled approach that is easily adapted to any constraints.
- Increasing accuracy in collecting and preserving skeletal and associated evidence.
- Understanding forces that may have disturbed the scene after it was created.
- Preventing postmortem damage to skeletal evidence.
- Recording environmental data for later use by entomologists, botanists, and other specialists.
- Effectively reconstructing events surrounding and subsequent to burial.
- Processing the scene in a thorough and professional manner with scientific experts.

7.1 General Principles of Archaeology

One of the principle distinctions of archaeology is examining change in societies over long periods, rather than the much shorter time scales of forensic investigation. Both types of evidence are susceptible to loss, alteration, or contamination, but archaeological evidence includes added changes brought about by long-term exposure to the burial environment. An understanding of the basic principles and terminology used in archaeology will be helpful when applying archaeological techniques to the forensic recovery of human remains.

7.1.1 Provenience and Context

Provenience refers to the exact location of an item in three-dimensional space, reflecting its latitude (north-south location), longitude (east-west location), and its vertical position (depth or elevation), as measured in meters (m) or centimeters (cm) (Renfrew and Bahn, 2000). An item that is still in the position in which it was originally deposited is said to be *in situ*.

Context, one of the most important terms in archaeology, is an object's exact place in time and space and its association and relationship with other items — that is, where it is and how it got there (Renfrew and Bahn, 2000). Context is the most easily lost of all potentially recoverable information. If objects are associated, they may be considered to have had a direct rather than circumstantial role in past events. Removing an object from its context without proper documentation destroys much of its potential to help reconstruct the behavior that placed it there.

Context and the association of objects are equally as important to forensic investigations as they have a legal importance in developing the reconstruction of events at a crime scene. Evidence loses most of its value if the context in which it is found is lost. This is extremely important considering that associated relationships between objects found at a crime scene are not always immediately apparent. In many cases, the common tactic is the rapid removal of the remains with brief notations on placement within the crime scene, resulting in the loss of the primary depositional context and incomplete scene reconstruction (Dirkmaat and Adovasio, 1997). Compromising the context of evidence can be as simple as elements of skeletonized remains being picked up, examined, or even removed from the scene to identify whether they are human. In some instances, the context of the scene may not always correspond with the evidence, as in cases where remains have been dumped.

7.1.2 Features

Unlike artifacts, which can be removed for later analysis, features have to be fully documented where they are found. In archaeology, a feature is an artifact that cannot be removed from the site (Renfrew and Bahn, 2000); for example, an animal burrow, posthole, trash pit, or man-made structure. Although archaeologists cannot remove a posthole from a site, they can learn much about the structure of the site and human behavior from documenting such artifacts.

In crime scenes with buried human remains, the grave can be viewed as a feature. It is part of the crime scene that cannot be removed, but, if excavated properly, valuable information regarding grave construction, geophysical characteristics, and other changes can be preserved (Hochrein, 1997a; 1997b; 2002).

7.1.3   Stratigraphy

For an archaeologist, stratigraphy is the primary basis for understanding buried materials, and provides the most direct information on how objects came to be buried. Stratigraphy is the analysis of the sequence of deposits in the soil that have formed through natural or human activities (Rapp and Hill, 1998). With time, the gradual buildup of these deposits form stratified layers one above the other. The strata, or layers, can be viewed as the pages in a book, while the stratigraphy is the story that is being told (Dirkmaat and Adovasio, 1997). Strata are distinguished by differences in color, texture, grain size, and composition. Depositions that form strata will vary due to climatic and environmental changes, as well as human intervention (e.g., building a road, digging a hole). Figure 7.1 shows an example of stratigraphy that was encountered and documented during a crime scene excavation. The various strata include differing soil layers as well as features, such as an old barn foundation (c), a cement floor (f), and a burial pit (h).

From a forensic perspective, digging a grave disturbs the natural stratification of the soil that inevitably makes the gravesite detectable either to

Figure 7.1   Example of a profile drawing of the stratigraphy associated with a burial (in order of deposition): (a) bedrock, (b) sterile soil layer, (c) barn foundation, (d) sandy soil layer, (e) barn wall, (f) cement floor, (g) debris layer, (h) burial pit, (i) chemical layer added to speed decomposition, (j) mixed fill removed from burial pit used to cover remains, (k) bricks used to fill hole in cement floor, (l) more mixed fill used to conceal burial, and (m) topsoil layer and surface vegetation.

the trained eye of the investigator or by using specialized equipment, such as ground penetrating radar. It is impossible to dig a hole and fill it exactly as it was without leaving evidence of disturbance within the soil layers. In most situations, when a perpetrator fills in a burial pit, the soil placed in the hole will consist of a mix of the various strata originally removed from the hole, and in some cases, other materials from the surrounding surface area. A burial pit is typically identified by a burial cut, which is the line of definition between the final fill of the grave and the undisturbed layers through which the burial has been dug.

When excavating, it is important to keep in mind that new strata, such as a layer of lime or various chemicals, may have been added in an attempt to conceal or aid in decomposition of the remains. It is also possible to detect whether or not the initial burial cut has been disturbed by looking for internal interruptions within the fill strata, such as those made by later removal or alteration of the grave contents.

7.1.4 Superposition and Relative Dating

The first, and in some ways most important, step in archaeological and forensic investigation involves ordering things into some type of sequence. Stratigraphy can aid in developing this sequence through the use of superposition. According to this principle, in undisturbed strata, older materials will tend to be at the bottom and more recent ones on top (Renfrew and Bahn, 2000). Since new depositions of soil are usually on top of preexisting layers, the relative date of layers can be determined; for example, an object closer to the surface will typically be more recent than the objects found beneath it.

The principle of superposition can easily be applied to forensic burials, particularly those with multiple individuals and associated evidence. When excavating these types of burials, bodies and objects that are on top can be interpreted as being the last to be placed in the grave. In opposition, those found on the bottom of the grave would have been placed in the burial first. The relative dating information acquired by careful excavation of human remains within the soil layers can supply invaluable information to the investigators. As an example, a bullet casing deposited on top of a grave must have been placed there after the grave was finished, but not before. Objects found in one of the layers below, above, or in relation to buried remains must have been deposited before, after, or at the time of burial. Objects found in any of the layers of a grave (i.e., the surface of the grave, above the body, the body itself and surrounding soil, and beneath the body), may yield physical evidence that should be interpreted relative to the layer in which it was recovered. This knowledge can help to interpret the events that occurred at a given crime scene; however, the investigator must keep in mind that these items are placed in analytical order based on their sequence of deposition, not on the exact age of the materials in the strata.

Looking back at Figure 7.1, we can develop a sequence in the burial of a body under the cement floor by using superposition. The cement floor

(f) was broken and the burial pit (h) was then dug for the body. After placing the body in the pit, a chemical substance (i) was dumped on top of the body and the pit was then filled in. Bricks (k) were placed in the cement break and then covered with the final infill of the burial pit (l). We know from superposition that the body was placed in the pit before the added chemical substance and that the bricks were placed in the burial pit before being covered over with a layer of soil. We can also determine that the surface layer (m) was deposited after the burial took place as it lies on top of the undisturbed debris layer (g) and the burial cut.

7.1.5   Geotaphonomy

Geotaphonomy involves the use of archaeological techniques to recognize specific geophysical characteristics and changes that affect the burial feature and the surrounding environment (Hochrein, 2002). Collection of this type of evidence focuses on the grave itself and may lead to identifying the initial method of digging as well as recognizing the source of any postdepositional disturbances.

7.1.5.1   Tool Marks

Tool marks left during the process of burial are routinely overlooked even though they may be well preserved above and below the ground surface. Understanding how the grave was dug and what tools were used may offer insight into the amount of planning and forethought that went into preparing the grave. Some soils, such as clays and silts, readily retain tool marks; however, sandy soils and gravels are too coarse and dry to hold the necessary details needed for evidence collection. Often soil and rock particles adhere to digging tools and may be matched through magnification to the soil profile from the burial cut.

It is important to prevent contamination and destruction of existing tool marks with excavation tools. In order to avoid contamination and destruction of tool marks, the outline of the burial should be clearly defined on the surface and excavations should begin inside of this outline with small hand tools. When the excavation level is below the areas containing the tool marks, small hand tools and brushes should be carefully used to expose the marks for photography and casting. Castings of tool marks are typically made using dental gypsum and a mason's board to form a negative image of the tool mark. These casts often show notches and striae that have formed on the metal edges of the digging tool and can be matched with the exact tool or the proper class of tool used. Paint chips from the surface of the tool that may not be evident to the naked eye may also be recovered in the casting process.

7.1.5.2   Bioturbation

Bioturbation is the mixing, displacement, or modification of the position of materials in the soil (Micozzi, 1991). Plants and animals cause the most recognizable forms of bioturbation and can sometimes lead to the determination of burial season or year.

Scavenging animals tend to displace evidence when digging and will often carry skeletal elements through their tunnels back to their burrows. It is sometimes necessary to follow these tunnels to recover certain elements. Root networks from plants can either hold together or displace burial evidence. One commonly overlooked form of botanical evidence is the slice or cut marks in roots that were caused by digging tools during the burial process (Bock and Norris, 1997; Willey and Heilman, 1987).

7.1.5.3 Sedimentation

Water flowing over or through the burial may result in sedimentation of eroded silts or the formation of fissures. The drying out of silts may result in cracking patterns that change during wet and dry phases. The patterns that form can be affected by settling within the burial pit over time and at times are used to locate edges of a burial cut (Hochrein, 2002). Careful excavation of these silt layers may also be used to determine the number of rain events that led to layer deposition and may be matched with local weather records to estimate the duration of burial. Fissures from water flows can run through a burial, and small bones or objects can fall into deeper layers below the remains. These should be excavated to possibly recover any missing skeletal elements.

7.1.5.4 Compaction and Depression

Compaction marks are familiar elements in most forensic scenes and include impressions from such things as shoes, tires, kneeling, and the backs of shovel blades used to pack the fill on top of a burial. Areas of extreme compaction can contain soil that is hard enough to preserve clothing impressions, particularly cloth such as denim, wool, or other types of heavy, coarse-weave fabrics. All of these marks are usually photographed or cast to preserve their details so that they may be later used in identification of a suspect.

Depressions are changes in the surface contours of the soil and are usually described as being either primary or secondary. Primary depressions form when the freshly dug fill settles in the burial pit, while secondary depressions occur when soil settles as a result of the release of gases and the collapse of the abdominal region during decomposition (Killam, 1990). Secondary depressions do not always form and can be dependent on the position of the body during burial. Eroded holes made by scavenging animals over the burial are commonly mistaken for a secondary depression.

7.2 Process of Burial

During the initial digging of a grave, the soil that is removed will normally be placed adjacent to the burial and on top of any vegetation that may be present. The soil from the grave then becomes intermixed with existing topsoil, plants, and surface material. This entire area is referred to as the burial site. On average, assuming that the original intent is to bury the body in the extended position, the dimensions of the disturbed area will be at least twice as wide as the body, due to displaced soil next to the grave, and approximately the same length as the body. The terrain, type of soil, and effort expended in digging the grave, will influence how deep the burial will be. In general, hand dug graves are usually as deep as is necessary to conceal the body due to the fact that digging a hole of this size is physically demanding and time consuming.

When filling a grave, there will generally be some original soil that cannot be returned to the burial pit due to the soil compaction being disturbed and the volume of the body displacing a portion of the original fill. The excess soil is usually scattered around the edges of the burial or left with no attempt to level the surface with the surrounding area, resulting in a small ridge or rise next to the burial (Duncan, 1983). Naturally, there is a high probability that geotaphonomic changes will occur at the site, making the appearance of the burial differ significantly over time.

Many offenders will go to great lengths to dispose of their victims in a manner intended to avoid detection, however, according to Killam (1990), most individuals will dispose of bodies in one of two ways: those that are dumped quickly within an area little-known or unknown to the perpetrator; and those that are deposited in an area where the landscape is well-known through ownership, holidays, or frequent visits. Killam (1990) also states that some 90% of victims are recovered downhill to facilitate carrying or deposition from vehicular access points along roadways.

7.3   Description of Burials

Knowledge of some of the main varieties of burials encountered in the archaeological record can provide useful information when excavating human remains in a forensic context. In some cases, bones may be found as singular elements and not as complete burials. This may be the result of animal scavenging where teeth, small bones, or bone fragments become mixed with refuse or organic material (Haglund, 1997a; 1997b; see Chapter 3). There are generally four types of burials that may be encountered in an archaeological and forensic investigation: primary, secondary, multiple, and cremations (Dirkmaat and Adovasio, 1997). However, surface deposits and disturbed burials are also quite common.

7.3.1   Surface Deposit

A surface deposit occurs when the remains are left to decompose on the surface of the ground (Burns, 1998). It is very common for this type of burial to be scattered or destroyed by animal scavenging, insect activity, or erosion. However, information can still be recovered from the context of the remains. Careful investigation of the scattered remains and the identification of

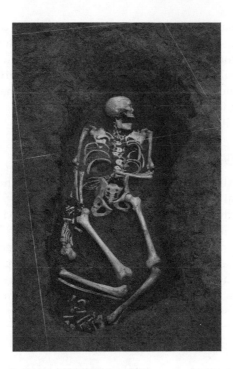

Figure 7.2   Skeletal elements from a primary burial found in an anatomical position during a simulated forensic scene investigation.

taphonomic processes may aid in establishing the postmortem interval and may reflect the various environmental conditions under which the displacement occurred (Haglund and Sorg, 1997).

7.3.2   Primary Burials

In a primary burial, the body remains in its original deposited position and the context of the burial has not been disturbed (Roksandic, 2002; Sharer and Ashmore, 2003). When excavated, the bones will appear to be articulated; that is, all the bones will remain in correct anatomical position in relation to one another as if soft tissues were still present (shown in Figure 7.2). The presumption is that the relationships of the articulations have not been altered since the decomposition of the soft tissue. Primary burials are the most common type of burial encountered in a forensic context.

7.3.3   Disturbed Burials

In a forensic investigation, the identification of disturbances is crucial in understanding the burial context. A disturbed burial is one that has been altered at some point after the initial burial, but not necessarily moved to a new place (Burns, 1998; Sharer and Ashmore, 2003). Burrowing animals, erosion, heavy equipment, or human activity are typical causes of burial disturbance. In most cases, a few of the skeletal elements may be disarticulated or missing while the remaining elements are preserved in their original anatomical position. Skeletal elements missing due to erosion or animal activity may be recovered by tracing the routes of removal. Identification of human activity, such as someone returning to the burial to remove or add specific items, may play an important role in later legal aspects of the investigation.

7.3.4 Secondary Burials

A secondary burial consists of skeletal elements that have been removed from their original burial location by human activity, and deposited in another location, thus disturbing their original context (Roksandic, 2002; Sharer and Ashmore, 2003). If sufficient time has elapsed to allow for complete decomposition of the soft tissue, the bones removed from the primary burial will not remain in an articulated or anatomical position unless purposefully placed in this fashion. Consequently, the secondary grave commonly consists of a jumbled arrangement of skeletal remains. In addition, it is not unusual for some skeletal elements to be missing.

7.3.5 Multiple Burials

A multiple burial consists of a single grave containing the remains of two or more individuals (Burns, 1998; Sharer and Ashmore, 2003). The individuals may either have been buried all at once as a primary deposit, or as a combination of primary and disturbed burials due to reentering an existing grave to deposit additional remains. Although multiple burials are occasionally found in a forensic context, the most common occurrence is in cases of human rights violations where many individuals will be deposited into one large burial pit (Haglund, 2002; Schmitt, 2002; Simmons, 2002; Skinner et al., 2002; Stover and Ryan, 2001).

7.3.6 Cremations or Thermal Damage to Skeletal Remains

Cremation is a process that uses intense heat to rapidly reduce a body to ashes and small bone fragments (Iserson, 2001). Bodies are typically burned prior to burial or within the grave and may be charred, or partially, incompletely, or completely burned depending on the intensity of the fire to which the body was exposed (Correia and Beattie, 2002). The remains may be mixed in with other elements of the burial (for example, clothing or wood), left as a surface deposit, or held in some type of container.

In a forensic investigation, forensic anthropologists examine cremated remains originating as the result of criminal activity and also as a result of normal cultural practices when a loved one dies. In the case where remains are cremated as the result of the perpetrator deliberately trying to dispose of the remains, the remains will most likely range from charred to incompletely burnt as it takes extremely high temperatures (above 1600°C/2912°F) to destroy bone (Iserson, 2001). It is almost impossible to completely destroy all evidence of a body through burning. Because of this fact, cremations that result from crematoriums are normally reduced to very small particles, depending on the type of processor used to reduce the remains.

7.4 Position and Orientation of the Body

Position is best described through the relationship of legs, arms, and head to each other and to the trunk of the body (Ubelaker, 1989). The description should relate to only the body with no reference to the burial pit, compass directions, or any other natural features. According to Ubelaker, "it should be as if the body is floating in space" (1989:16). Recording the orientation of the remains is also extremely important. Orientation is the direction in which the head lies in relation to the body's central axis and should be recorded in directional terms using a compass or natural as well as man-made features, but preferably in a combination of all these reference points (Ubelaker, 1989).

In a primary burial, the body may be described as being in an extended, flexed, or semi-flexed position as shown in Figure 7.3. An extended position indicates that the legs are straight, forming a 180° angle with the trunk. The body can either be on its back or front. A flexed position signifies that the body is at an angle of 90° or less between the legs and the trunk, while semi-flexed refers to burials in which the angle of the legs is between 90° and 180° from the trunk.

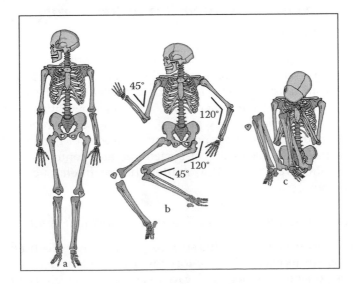

Figure 7.3 Examples of a primary burial in an: (a) extended position, (b) semiflexed position; and (c) flexed position. The semiflexed burial (b) shows an example of arms and legs at differing angles for the left and right sides.

It is extremely important to note how the arms and legs are positioned in relation to the rest of the body. For instance, arm and hand bones found to be positioned behind the body might indicate that the individual's hands had been bound behind the back when placed in the grave, even though traces of the ligature may have long since disintegrated. In addition, be sure to note whether both arms and legs are in the same position as it is very common to have the left and right sides differ. Also, treat the upper and lower parts of the extremities separately using position angles. The semi-flexed burial shown in Figure 7.3(b), for example, has differing angles for both right and left and upper and lower extremities. The left leg would be recorded as having a 120° pelvic angle, while the lower leg has a 45° angle. The lower right arm has a 120° angle while the lower left arm has a 45° angle. When recording the position of the head, be sure to note whether it is facing left, right, or forward and whether it is extended backward or is compressed toward the chest.

In a forensic investigation, the body may be found in any position, and in many cases is directly related to the size of the burial pit. The position of the body may also give some indication as to what postmortem state the body was in when placed in the grave. If the body was in full rigor it is unlikely that the individual would be placed in a grave in a tightly flexed position. A tightly flexed position would indicate that the individual was placed in the grave prior to the onset of full rigor or after rigor had broken. The onset and length of time that rigor lasts is dependent on multiple variables (such as age, sex, physical condition, musculature) but is particularly influenced by the ambient temperature (Ludwig, 2002).

7.5   Archaeological Approaches to Recovering Human Remains

As most forensic archaeologists can attest, every crime scene involving human remains is different, and as such the archaeological techniques used to excavate a site must be adapted to each particular scene. Flexibility is key when evaluating the environment and working conditions that will be encountered during the recovery process. Although each scene is different, the general methodology of excavation and removal of remains is similar. Forensic archaeology makes use of systematic and controlled approaches that can be effectively applied no matter the condition or context of the recovery scene.

7.5.1   Removing Surface Remains and Associated Evidence

Human remains that are left on the surface are likely to be disturbed in some manner prior to recovery. Every effort must be made to recover as much evidence as possible, especially in locations where the terrain is difficult and scattering is extensive. Recording and mapping is also important in these instances to better understand and recreate the events that took place during the postmortem interval.

7.5.1.1 Step #1 — Examining the Recovery Area and Establishing Spatial Controls

Typically, a forensic investigator will determine the perimeter of the scene and crime scene personnel will carry out all initial documentation of evidence. However, in some cases, the forensic archaeologist will assist in this process. It is recommended that in either instance, detailed descriptions of the scene and a general overall sketch be completed prior to any recovery actions.

- Appraise any constraints on recovery (e.g., landscape, weather, time limits, manpower, and equipment availability) and plan adaptations of archaeological methods for recovery.
- Determine the extent of the area associated with main surface site and designate the perimeter of the recovery area.
- Establish a single, restricted route of access to and from the main surface site and recovery area.
- Construct a baseline and datum for mapping surface levels and evidence in the recovery area. In some instances, multiple grids may be needed in different areas of evidence concentrations.
- Record and map any geotaphonomic and material evidence on the surface of the recovery area, avoiding the main surface site at this time. Move from the outer perimeter inward in a 1 m spiral pattern to avoid disturbing or damaging any evidence that may be located in the central portion of the area or the main site.
- After the evidence within the recovery area has been recorded and mapped, construct a reference grid over and around the main surface site (Figure 7.4). Record and map any surface evidence that might be disturbed during the next step when the main surface site is cleared.

Figure 7.4 Constructing a grid over a suspected burial at a simulated crime scene.

It is recommended that during the recording and mapping of evidence within the recovery area, a metal detector be used to locate any bullet slugs or casings prior to their being found while screening removed materials. Bullet slugs or casings can easily be abraded by the screening process and damage the fine striations that may be used later for comparative evidence.

7.5.1.2   Step #2 — Exposing and Recording the Main Surface Site

Extreme care should be used when clearing and exposing the surface as small bones, teeth, and hair tend to be scraped up in the debris. These items can be recovered if the material is screened and sorted properly.

- Remove any loose debris (e.g., leaves, sticks, trash) from surface of the grid area one square at a time; screen or sort through any loose debris.
- Remove any surface vegetation to expose the remains for recording and mapping; screen or sort through any surface vegetation. Take care to record any debris or vegetation that may have been purposefully placed over the remains as this may indicate intent to conceal the body.
- Record and map all exposed elements and associated evidence.

7.5.1.3   Step #3 — Removing Surface Remains

- If elements are stratified or if there is more than one individual present, treat the remains as if they were in layers, recording and mapping each layer prior to its removal. If elements are partially embedded in the ground surface, be sure that each element is carefully loosened from the surrounding soil before attempting removal.
- During removal, any entomological or botanical samples that are related to the remains should be taken.
- Once all of the evidence has been removed from the grid area, a soil sample should be taken from the ground directly below the remains within the main site and the ground surface should be gone over with a metal detector, if available.
- The ground surface should be scraped down to sterile soil and the removed soil should be screened.
- After the recovery area has been double-checked for any remaining details, all materials should be removed from the site except for the datum.

7.5.2   Removing Buried Remains and Associated Evidence

Burials have many of their own characteristics that if excavated properly can provide vital information. Recognizing evidence depends on systematic and careful removal of the burial fill from the original walls and floor of the burial cut. Extreme care should be taken at each step of the process to ensure proper recording and mapping of evidence with nothing being moved or removed without first noting its position and marking it for later identification. Photographs should be used as backup to the written record and not as the principal source of information. The excavation of human remains generally follows a series of six steps that are outlined as follows (Dirkmaat and Adovasio, 1997; Morse et al., 1983; Skinner and Lazenby, 1983):

7.5.2.1 Step #1 — Examining the Recovery Area and Establishing Spatial Controls

This step follows a process similar to the initial step of surface recovery presented previously. Any precautions mentioned earlier in the recovery of surface remains should also be observed when working with buried remains.

- Appraise any constraints on recovery (e.g., landscape, weather, time limits, manpower, equipment availability) and plan adaptations of archaeological methods for recovery.
- Determine the extent of the area associated with burial site and designate the perimeter of the recovery area.
- Establish a single, restricted route of access to and from the burial site and recovery area.
- Construct a baseline and datum for mapping surface levels and evidence in the recovery area. In some instances, a grid may be needed in an area of evidence concentration not involving the burial site.
- Record and map any geotaphonomic and material evidence on the surface of the recovery area, avoiding the burial site at this time. Move from the outer perimeter inward in a 1 m spiral pattern to avoid disturbing or damaging any evidence that may be located in the central portion of the area or the burial site. If available, a metal detector should be used over the recovery area after evidence has been recorded and mapped.
- After the surface evidence within the recovery area has been removed, construct a reference grid over and around the burial site (Figure 7.4). Establish a secondary datum within the reference grid for the burial site if needed. Record and map any surface evidence that might be disturbed during the next step when the burial site surface is cleared.

7.5.2.2 Step #2 — Identifying and Examining the Burial Cut

- Remove loose debris (e.g., leaves, sticks, trash) and surface vegetation from the surface of the grid area one square at a time using small hand tools; screen and sort through all materials removed from the surface of the burial site. Take care to record any debris or vegetation that may have been purposefully placed over the remains as this may indicate intent to conceal the body.
- Scrape surface soils (no deeper than 1 cm) into dustpans and buckets for screening. Keep materials from different grid squares separate

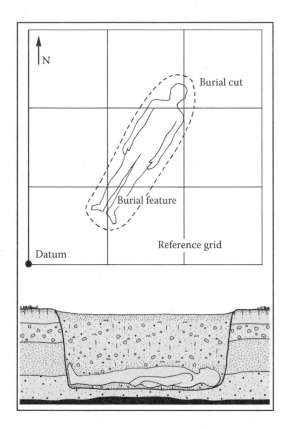

Figure 7.5   Example of a reference grid and profile of an exposed burial cut.

during screening so any associated evidence that is found can be placed in reference to other items.

- Determine the edges of the burial cut by changes in soil color or other identifiers such as cracks, depressions, or tool marks.
- Clear the entire grid area and map the surface and the edges of the burial cut, and any exposed remains or associated evidence, before moving on to Step #3.

Figure 7.5 shows an example of a reference grid and profile with the burial cut exposed.

7.5.2.3   Step #3 — Excavating the Burial Feature

In this step, there are two possible ways to proceed with excavation depending on whether the edges of the burial cut can be identified. If the edges of the burial cut are evident, it is recommended that investigators excavate the burial feature, meaning that the removal of soil will primarily occur within the defined burial cut (Connor and Scott, 2001) (Figure 7.6). If the burial cut is

Figure 7.6 Author Sandra Wheeler demonstrates the proper procedures when excavating a burial feature.

ignored during the recovery process, there is every probability that materials from surrounding soil layers can contaminate the burial and be mistakenly introduced as evidence.

If the edges of the burial cut are not clearly defined by color differences or other characteristics (this is possible in certain geographical locations where soil will homogenize after a certain amount of time has passed), proceed in the following manner:

- Working from a corner and across the grid, remove soil in 5 cm layers in one grid square at a time using a trowel, keeping all grid squares at the same depth. The trowel should be held at an angle with the bottom edge on the soil surface and the top edge angled outward, and should always be brought toward you in a scraping motion to avoid digging holes in the ground. Never use the point of the trowel to remove soil.
- Screen all soil from each layer removed from the burial feature, keeping materials from each grid square separate during screening. Determine the layer depth for any soil being screened so associated evidence that is recovered can be placed in reference to other items.
- Record and map any artifacts or evidence encountered before moving on to remove the next layer.
- If the burial cut is encountered, proceed with the excavation as described below; if remains or any containers or wrappings are encountered, move on to Step #4 for exposing and recording the remains.

Excavation of a burial feature with a defined cut should proceed as follows:

- Initially, only one half of the burial feature should be excavated until remains or any containers or wrappings are encountered. This creates a profile of the position and orientation of the body within the burial feature that can be clearly shown in drawings and photographs (see Figure 7.7). Once the profile has been recorded, the other half of the burial may be excavated in the same manner.
- Excavation should begin in the grid square over the center of the burial feature and move out toward the edges of the burial cut, leaving a 3- to 5-cm margin of fill soil along the cut line. This allows for the later exposure of the burial feature walls and floor, thereby increasing the possibility of preserving geotaphonomic evidence such as tool marks.
- The fill soil should be removed in 5 cm layers from one square at a time, keeping all grid squares being excavated at the same depth. If the remains are thought to be in an extended position, use extreme care when removing soil from the ends as one will contain the skull and the other the feet, both of which can easily be disturbed or damaged if the depth of the grave is unknown.
- Screen all soil from each layer removed from the burial feature, keeping materials from each grid square separate during screening. Determine the layer depth for any soil being screened so associated evidence that is recovered can be placed in reference to other items.
- After the first 20- to 30-cm of soil is removed, carefully excavate the remaining fill against the burial cut line. Use small hand tools and brushes to preserve any tool marks that may be present.
- Record and map any artifacts or evidence encountered before moving on to remove the next layer (Figures 7.7 and 7.8). Note any differing soil types by placing markers in a feature wall for later recording in a profile drawing.
- Once remains or any containers or wrappings are encountered, move on to the next step for exposing and recording the remains.

Never stand in a burial until the exact burial position is known and the remains have been completely exposed, as it is easy to crush delicate bones or objects that may be associated with the burial. It is usually better to excavate lying on the side of the grave or on planks laid across the exposed burial cut; however, planks should only be used after any tool mark evidence has been recorded. If the depth of the burial increases to the point at which it impedes proper excavation (i.e., at depths where the excavator is at risk of falling into the feature), it may be necessary to remove one long side of the burial feature in stages to create a working platform as excavation progresses (as shown in Figure 7.9). The platform height should always be higher than the surface being excavated, and it should only be lowered after the wall of the burial cut has been recorded at each stage.

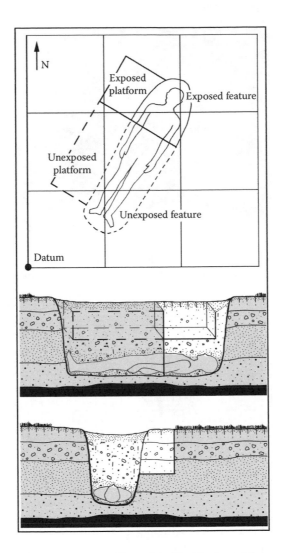

Figure 7.7 A reference grid and profile with half of the burial feature exposed (using a platform).

Soils that are heavily compacted or waterlogged (for example, clays, river sediments, bogs, retention pond materials) may be washed through a fine screen to help recover fragments or other associated evidence. This may be done with water from light-pressure hoses or by dumping buckets of water over the materials to be screened. Care must be taken to avoid overflow and people screening the materials must be alert for any evidence that may float in the water.

7.5.2.4 Step #4 — Exposing the Remains
The process of gradually uncovering the remains *in situ* is designed to preserve the posture of the body and the relationship of any associated

Figure 7.8   Orange County homicide detective Dave Clarke takes depth measurements from the datum on exposed clothing and skeletal elements at a simulated crime scene.

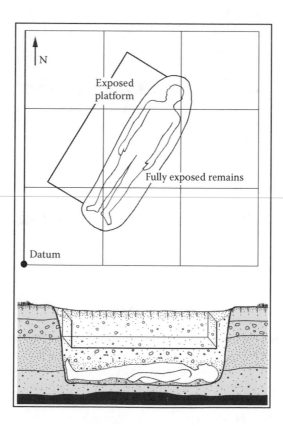

Figure 7.9   A reference grid and profile of a burial feature with the remains fully exposed.

Figure 7.10   Author Sandra Wheeler and students expose and clean the skeleton for mapping and photography.

evidence, such as wrappings around the remains, containers, or any materials added to the remains prior to filling the burial. All disturbed soil within the burial feature should be excavated to expose the entire body, container, or wrappings (as shown in Figure 7.9).

- Working carefully with small hand tools, expose the entire remains across the grid area (Figure 7.10). Use wood tools or plastic spoons and brushes when working close to the bone surface to avoid leaving any tool marks from excavation. Always work from exposed areas toward unexposed areas to prevent damaging remains or additional evidence that may be at different levels. Excavation notes should contain details of any damage that may occur during recovery to avoid any confusion about tool marks on the remains at a later date.
- If containers or wrappings are encountered, these should be treated as any other layer within the burial and excavated with care as additional evidence may be collected from the folds or surfaces of the materials.
- With the exception of smaller items that may impede excavation and that have been recorded and mapped, nothing should be removed at this point.
- When excavating in areas around the abdominal and pelvic regions, extreme caution should be used, as fetal remains may be present in females. These are very fragile and expert handling is recommended (refer to section 7.8).

Figure 7.11   Author Sandra Wheeler and students record all measurements of the skeleton.

- Entomological and soil samples should be taken from the thoracic and abdominal cavity areas prior to fully exposing the area around the pelvis and lumbar vertebrae; soil in these areas tends to contain insects and other chemical evidence not easily detected in the field.
- The following points on the body should be mapped and have depths taken from the datum: skull, pelvic bones, knees, elbows, shoulders, hands and feet, and any associated objects found with the remains.
- All remains and associated artifacts should be fully recorded and mapped before moving on to Step #5 (Figure 7.11).

Extreme care should be taken when exposing the remains as many important items may be overlooked if not brought to mind during recovery. Such things as contact lenses, pacemakers, prosthetic implants, and items associated with surgical procedures are quite common in populations today and most can play a role in the identification of an individual. Any unidentified objects found in association with the individual should be kept as evidence until a pathologist can review the materials.

7.5.2.5   Step #5 — Removing the Remains

The following process largely refers to skeletal remains but can be adapted to remains found in various stages of decomposition:

- To minimize disturbance and damage, feet and hands should be removed first, then work from the lower legs toward the chest. Arms and ribs should be removed prior to the pelvis and vertebrae, and the skull should be the final element recovered. However, if the skeletal remains are not in a supine position, the sequence and direction of removal may vary considerably. In cases such as this, skeletal elements that overlap one another should be removed and recorded in layers using the above order when possible.

- Take great care in removing the skull and mandible so that the teeth remain in their sockets and no damage is caused to the skull. Do not pick the skull up by the eye orbits or any other open area (the bones in these areas are very fragile and will easily break); gently cradle it in both hands and lift with equal pressure on the fingertips and palms of your hands. Also be aware that scalp and facial hair may have slipped from position and may be preserved under the skull or around the lower facial region.

- When removing the skull, pelvis, and shoulder blades, be aware of possible soft tissue preservation or clothing between these bones and the soil layers below the body. Also, be sure to check for any jewelry, such as necklaces, earrings, rings, or bracelets, which may have slipped into the surrounding soil.

- Remains held in anatomical position by preserved clothing, such as shirts, pants, shoes or socks, should be removed as a unit and be investigated under more controlled conditions. Any skeletal elements not contained within clothing should be removed and packaged separately from those contained in preserved clothing.

- A recording sheet of all skeletal elements removed should be completed at this time to account for any possible missing elements prior to moving on to Step #6.

7.5.2.6 Step #6 — Excavating the Burial Cut

The burial feature floor is often mistakenly thought to be the point at which the evidence stops, but, at times it can contain some of the most important evidence within the burial context. Many items or materials may have penetrated the floor in a visually unrecognizable manner, for example, bullets fired through a victim or permeating toxic chemicals added to enhance decomposition. The following process will aid in the detection of any remaining evidence within the burial feature:

- Record soil types and depths of each soil layer and record the depth of any evidence markers placed in the feature wall for the profile drawing of the burial.

- Collect a soil sample from the floor of the feature that includes soil from a few centimeters under the floor surface.

- Using a small hand tool or trowel, scrape all surfaces of the feature and screen for evidence that may have been embedded in the walls or under the body. If possible, a metal detector should also be used over the floor at this time. Scrape the floor of the feature until sterile soil is reached.

- Follow any water fissures caused by erosion, cracks, or animal burrows to recover displaced remains or associated evidence. Map any evidence recovered in relation to the burial feature.

- Once everything has been recorded and collected, determine whether the burial feature should be backfilled at this time. When backfilling, the feature should be filled with the removed soil and leveled with the surface.
- All materials should be removed from the burial site except for the datum.

If a secondary datum was established for excavation, a length of metal rod or pipe, scored with the datum height above the ground surface, can be used to indicate the original position of the datum. The rod or pipe can then be driven into the ground flush with the surface and can easily be recovered using a metal detector, if needed at a later date.

7.6   Packaging and Storage of Human Skeletal Remains

During removal from the burial feature, identifying marks should never be placed directly on the bone. Each bone should be identified inside and outside of its package by a tag noting its precise location coordinates either on a control-point or grid-mapping system. Any evidence numbering system that is used by the forensic investigation team should be duplicated in the excavation notes and on the tags for each package to prevent any confusion about identification at a later date.

Packaging guidelines for skeletal human remains free of soft tissue are simple: everything should go in paper bags. Buried remains are inevitably going to have some moisture, and packaging in plastic bags or aluminum foil does not allow the moisture to evaporate and will promote the growth of fungus and mold. In addition, the moisture may accelerate the breakdown of skeletal material (Skinner and Lazenby, 1983). Place a tag with the pertinent information about the bone inside the paper bag before sealing it shut.

The opening of each paper bag should be folded over at least twice and then stapled or taped shut to prevent bones from falling out during transport. Small bags can be placed inside large ones, which in turn can be loaded and sealed into clean cardboard boxes or body bags. Padding should be used between packages to prevent breakage and care should be taken to avoid stacking packages on top of one another when placing them in boxes. Each bag should be clearly labeled with, at a minimum, information regarding the content, location, case information, and investigator's name. If necessary, crime scene evidence tape and the investigator's signature can be placed over the folded opening of the bag for purposes of chain-of-custody. Each agency may also have its own mandate for preserving evidence, and if this is the case, then those guidelines should be followed.

The skull and mandible should be packaged separately from the other remains to prevent any damage and to contain any soil or other deposits found inside the cranium. This will also prevent any teeth from becoming lost during transport. Pelvic bones should also be packaged separately from other elements, taking special precautions with the pubic surfaces.

When possible, bones from the left and right sides, such as the ribs, hands, and feet, should be bagged separately.

Remains that are in advanced states of decomposition with wet soft tissue still remaining should be packaged so fluids do not leak during transport. The most efficient method is to wrap the body parts in a cotton sheet or other disposable lint-free material, then place them into a zippered body bag. Do not seal any plastic bag with tissues inside unless the odor is extreme, and even then, only during the time required for transport. Any associated clothing, wrappings, or containers from the burial should accompany the remains for further investigation.

7.7 Recovery of Fleshed Remains

There are instances when the degree of human decomposition is such that a different type of approach may be necessary; however, partially decomposed remains should be excavated using the same systematic and controlled approaches as described previously. Modification of the process usually occurs when the remains are exposed, and minor adjustments may be necessary to preserve as much of the original burial environment as possible when removing the remains for investigation under more controlled conditions.

When the majority of a body is exposed, there is a tendency to want to pull it free from the burial feature. There is a danger that weakened articulations, especially the knees, ankles, neck, wrists, or fingers, may separate, leaving disarticulated portions in the burial feature. This presents the potential for losing important pieces of soft tissue evidence, such as fingernails, fingerprints, and defense wounds or ligature marks. The best method for removal is to completely expose the remains, work around and loosen the areas where the remains are in contact with the floor of the burial feature, then lift the remains as a whole, preferably with a stretcher board support or with many individuals lifting at the same time. Once the body is removed, excavations can continue with investigation of the burial cut and any associated evidence.

7.8 Recovery of Juvenile Remains

The challenges involved in locating and excavating juvenile remains are much greater than those typically encountered in forensic investigation. This is principally due to their differential preservation and misidentification, or inadequate excavation techniques used in recovery. The environment and scavenging animals also easily displace juvenile remains, especially those of infants. Because of their size and number, it is likely that many skeletal elements from juveniles will be missed during the search and recovery processes unless properly identified and collected.

Infant and fetal remains could easily be misidentified as items that would typically be seen in a recovery area, such as twigs, pebbles, small animal skeletons, or the remains of a chicken dinner. The number of bones present can also be misleading, as elements often appear fragmentary and nonhuman in nature. These small skeletal elements are also extremely fragile and do not have the rigidity and hardness often associated with bone. It is crucial that great care be taken when processing a recovery site that might involve a juvenile. Investigators should work with someone well versed in juvenile osteology, ensuring the proper collection, preservation, documentation, and analysis of this type of evidence.

7.9   Recovery of Burnt Remains

The nature of burnt remains differs greatly from normal skeletal remains. The temperature of the fire and the length of time that a body is exposed to the fire will determine the appearance of the remains. When exposed to high temperatures, bone will change color, crack and warp, and even explode. Burnt bone is unlikely to have much potential for molecular and chemical analysis, though DNA may still be recovered in some instances (Redsicker and O'Connor, 1996; Weedn, 1997).

Cremated or burnt remains can turn up in all sorts of contexts but most are encountered in surface and shallow burials or in containers (Fairgrieve and Molto, 1994; Murad, 1998). Burnt bones are extremely fragile and must be disturbed as little as possible. A common methodology in fire investigation is to rake through the coals to recover as much as possible as quickly as possible, thus disturbing any relationship that existed between the bones and any other associated evidence. In cases such as this, we recommend that a forensic anthropologist who is familiar with fire recovery techniques and bone identification be used to recover evidence of this type.

With a substantial amount of information still able to be gathered from *in situ* burnt human remains, a forensic anthropologist specializing in burnt remains could (Correia and Beattie, 2002; Dirkmaat, 2002; King and King, 1989):

- Identify nonhuman vs. human remains.
- Establish whether the remains were burned on location or burned elsewhere and redeposited.
- Determine the number of victims found in the fire debris and their locations and orientations during the fire.
- Increase the accuracy in the collection of evidence and minimize the damage to bone fragments.
- Aid in the scene reconstruction with details on fire intensity, duration, and patterns of body and tissue alteration or destruction due to fire exposure.

chapter 8

Forensic Archaeological Case Study

As all of the authors are practicing forensic archaeologists and forensic anthropologists, we thought it would be useful to include a case study that illustrates all the different forensic archaeological procedures that we have outlined in this book. This case outlines the techniques used to locate and recover the skeletal remains of Lisa Brighton.*

Fourteen-year-old Lisa Brighton was last seen on May 25, 1987 walking near a convenience store with Wayne Smith. At this time, Smith was already under investigation for the rape of another woman. Formal charges were brought against Smith for this rape and he was sentenced to three years in jail. While Smith was serving his sentence, investigators were building a case against him for the suspected murder of Lisa.

In 1991, Smith was released from prison. Since investigators suspected him in the disappearance and murder of Lisa, they assigned officers to tail Smith in the hope that he would return to Lisa's burial site. One afternoon, Smith escaped the scrutiny of his observers, and during this time he did return to Lisa's grave, dug up her skeleton, and proceeded to remove certain skeletal elements. Smith had conducted research while in prison as to what skeletal elements were typically used for identifying an individual. If Lisa's skeleton was ever to be discovered, Smith wanted to ensure that investigators could not identify her. Of course, this was before the acceptance of DNA as a viable method for identification.

Although they never discovered the location of Lisa's remains, investigators were able to amass enough information to arrest and charge Smith with Lisa's murder six years after her disappearance. Prosecutors convinced a jury of Smith's guilt, without the discovery of Lisa's body, and he was sentenced to death.

In September of 2001, 14 years after Lisa's disappearance, a rare and highly unusual plea deal was arranged in which Smith agreed to confess to Lisa's

---

* Names have been changed to protect the identity of the victim and her family.

Figure 8.1   The wooded lot identified by Smith as the spot where he buried Lisa Brighton.

murder and reveal the location of her remains. For his cooperation Smith's death sentence would be converted to a life sentence without parole. At this time, Smith revealed the details of Lisa's murder and also told investigators about the time period in 1991 when he revisited Lisa's grave and removed certain skeletal elements. Under heavy security, Smith identified a wooded lot and the general area in which Lisa was buried (Figure 8.1). Although Smith could not pinpoint the exact location of the burial (as the vegetation had changed dramatically over 14 years), he revealed pertinent details that assisted investigators in their search plan. Smith indicated that he had buried Lisa in a shallow natural depression, with her head beside the root of a large tree. At the time of Lisa's burial, the area around the wooded lot was under heavy construction, and Smith said that he took large strips of metal from the construction site and placed them over her body. He then used a metal bucket to scoop dirt and cover the grave. When Smith returned to the burial site in 1991, he said that he lifted several of the metal pieces and removed Lisa's skull and her right leg in an effort to mask her identity. Smith's rationale for removing these skeletal elements was that Lisa's teeth could be used to make a dental identification, and he removed her leg because when Lisa was younger she had been in a serious car accident that required her right leg to be reconstructed, therefore leaving behind signs of trauma that might be used to identify her.

Investigators, including authors Dupras, Wheeler, and Williams, proceeded to search the area using multiple search techniques. First, the area was searched using a strip or line search method. During this time, investigators looked for any signs of burial depression, and also for the descriptors that Smith had mentioned. After the visual search was conducted, a metal detector was used to scan the area, since Smith had described that he used strips of metal to cover Lisa's body. Survey flags were used to mark any metal detector alerts. The last

Figure 8.2 After completing the search, the initial work area was delineated by survey tape. Investigators then cleared the surface of any debris. Survey flags mark the areas where the metal detector made alerts.

search technique used was a cadaver dog. The combination of all these search techniques indicated a particular area within the wooded lot. At this point, the area was marked with flagging tape and the surface was cleared of debris (Figure 8.2). All the debris removed from the surface was then screened, so that no possible evidence would be overlooked (Figure 8.3).

Figure 8.3 Author Lana Williams and crime scene investigators screen all the debris from the surface.

Figure 8.4   After clearing the area, a grid was set up over the area. Letters and numbers along the edges identify each grid square.

After clearing the surface, a grid was set up over the area (Figure 8.4) and excavation proceeded. It was not long before several strips of metal (Figure 8.5) were revealed. At each stage, the scene was documented with photos in addition to the plan and section maps that were drawn (see Figure 8.6 for a plan map of the metal strips). After the metal strips were documented and removed, excavations continued, and it was not long before the skeletal remains were revealed. One particularly important piece of evidence, a tooth, was discovered in the thoracic region (Figure 8.7). This tooth may have been missed had improper excavation techniques been employed. Although Smith had done

Figure 8.5   Excavation with trowels revealed several pieces of metal.

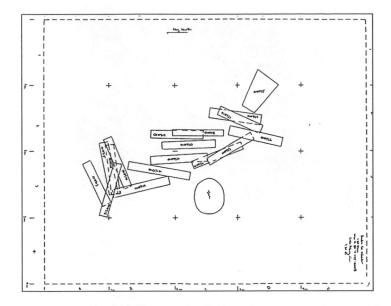

Figure 8.6   Plan map of the placement of the metal strips in reference to the large tree.

his best to remove all dental evidence, the tooth must have fallen out of the skull as he removed it, and since it was a similar color to the surrounding burial soil, he did not see it. Although not enough to make a dental identification, this tooth was later used for DNA analysis and was the one piece of evidence that enabled a positive identification of Lisa's remains.

Excavations proceeded until the entire skeleton was exposed (Figure 8.8). Once the skeleton was completely uncovered, some of the details of Smith's description were confirmed. For example, the position of the skeleton was

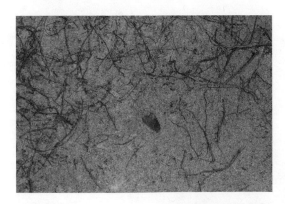

Figure 8.7   The single tooth recovered from Lisa Brighton's burial.

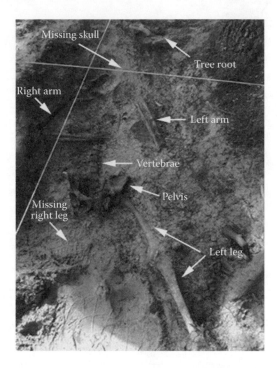

Figure 8.8   The exposed remains of Lisa Brighton. Note the missing skull and right leg.

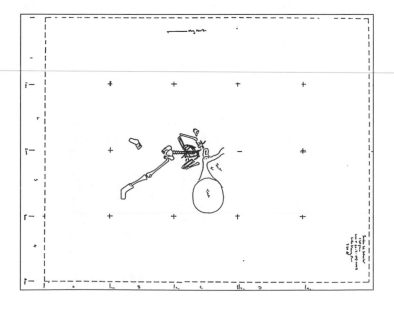

Figure 8.9   Plan map of the position of Lisa Brighton's skeleton in reference to the tree.

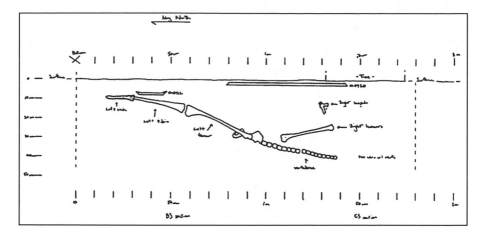

Figure 8.10   Profile or cross-sectional map of Lisa Brighton's remains.

such that the skull would have been beside or slightly under a large tree root. In addition, both the skull and the right leg were missing. Detailed plan and profile (cross-sectional) maps of the skeleton were produced before the skeleton was removed (Figure 8.9 and Figure 8.10). After removal, the skeleton was brought to the local medical examiner's office for further analysis. Lisa's remains were positively identified and then returned to her family. Smith's original death sentence was reduced to a life sentence.

chapter 9

Identification of Human Remains

A solid knowledge of human osteology is vital for the forensic anthropologist. Although forensic archaeologists may not have an expert knowledge of human skeletal anatomy, they should have a working knowledge so that they can distinguish the differences between human and nonhuman bone and also recognize human juvenile remains. We recognize that most field investigators, whether homicide detectives or crime scene personnel, will not have this specialized knowledge. The reason for including a section of human bone illustrations is not so the reader will become an expert in human osteology. This section is designed to help the reader create scene maps in which bones are illustrated and to provide help in understanding the terminology used in medical examiner, coroner, and forensic anthropology reports on skeletal material. This chapter is not meant to be used as a field guide for bone identification. The authors caution that the final identification of all skeletal material should be handled by the forensic anthropologist or medical examiner. Information such as sex, age at death, ancestry (that is, race), stature, pathology, and trauma should be determined by a forensic anthropologist; and therefore that information is not included in this book.

If further references are needed, there are several human anatomy books that contain sections on skeletal descriptions, and there are also books written by physical anthropologists that deal specifically with the human skeleton. These include *Human Osteology* by Tim White (2000), *Human Osteology: A Field and Laboratory Manual* by William Bass (1995), *Skeleton Keys* by Jeffrey Schwartz (1995), and *Anatomy and Biology of the Human Skeleton* by Gentry Steele and Claude Bramblett (1988). Since these texts are mainly concerned with adult skeletal morphology, the following can be used as reference for juvenile skeletal remains: *The Osteology of Infants and Children* by Brenda Baker, Tosha Dupras, and Matthew Tocheri (2005), *Developmental Juvenile Osteology* by Louise Scheuer and Sue Black (2000), and the condensed version of the previous book *The Juvenile Skeleton* by Louise Scheuer and Sue Black (2004).

9.1   Typical Skeletal Terminology Used in Forensic Reports

Forensic anthropologists, forensic archaeologists, and medical examiners typically use anatomical terminology to describe the location of skeletal trauma, pathology, or unique identifying characteristics. This section is designed to introduce terminology that the investigator may come across in such reports.

9.1.1   Terminology Associated with the Gross Morphology of Bone

Osteologists use broad terms to describe the gross morphological portions of the long bones. During the growth and development phase of mammalian bone, bones do not grow as one unit. For example, long bones, such as those of the arms and legs, will ultimately form from multiple bony elements. Each of the growth components has a specific name. The portion that makes up the shaft of the bone is referred to as the diaphysis, while the expanded end of the shaft is called the metaphysis and the ends of the bones are called epiphyses (Figure 9.1).

During the developmental phase of the long bones, the roughened, irregular ends of immature long bones are referred to as metaphyses. Between the ends of the shaft and the epiphyses, there is a cartilaginous center known as the epiphyseal growth plate or growth plate. This soft

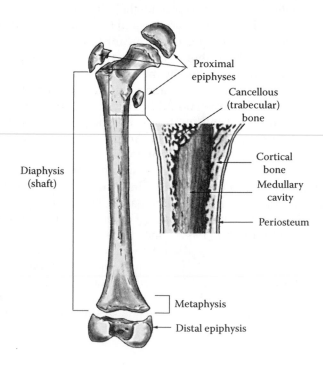

Figure 9.1   Parts and components of a long bone (posterior view of left femur).

tissue layer is responsible for bone growth at the ends of long bones. The very ends of the long bones which exist as separate bones until fusion occurs, are called the epiphyses (Figure 9.1).

In life, when long bones are articulated, the articular surface is covered with cartilage, and the bone surface under this cartilage is referred to as subchondral bone. The diaphysis of the long bone is made up of thick, dense cortical bone, while the ends are composed of cancellous or trabecular bone. The cortical bone of the diaphysis is covered by a fibrous soft tissue called the periosteum. The diaphysis of the long bone also has a feature called the nutrient foramen, which allows for the passage of bloods vessels and nerves into the bone. Each long bone also has a hollow center referred to as the medullary cavity. During life, this cavity is filled with yellow marrow (fat), and this area also houses the cells that produce red blood cells. See Table 9.1 for a summary of all the terminology associated with the gross morphology of the long bones.

Table 9.1 Descriptive Terms Associated with the Gross Morphology of the Long Bones

Nutrient foramen	A small hole or channel that penetrates the bone. It facilitates the entrance of blood vessels and nerves into the bone.
Periosteum	The soft tissue fibrous membrane that covers the bone.
Diaphysis	The shaft of the long bone.
Metaphysis	The growing and expanded portions of a long bone shaft between the diaphysis and the ends of the long bone where the growth plate is located and where the epiphyses will eventually fuse.
Epiphysis	Found at the ends of the long bones. During growth the epiphyses are initially separated from the metaphysis by a layer of cartilage that eventually ossifies and fuses the parts together.
Epiphyseal growth plate	The soft tissue structure (cartilage) located between the metaphysis and the epiphysis.
Medullary cavity	The inner cavity of the long bone, which in life provides storage for yellow marrow (fat) and is also the center for the production of red blood cells.
Subchondral bone	Bone located at the joint that is covered by cartilage during life.
Cortical bone	The dense, thickened outer layer of bone. Also referred to as compact bone.
Cancellous bone	The spongy or honeycomb structure of bone tissue typically found at the ends of long bones. Also referred to as trabecular or spongy bone.

9.1.2   Terminology Associated with Bone Features

Each bone of the skeleton has numerous associated features that are named according to their appearance. We have presented those terms that are most commonly associated with bony features, and those that are most likely to appear in forensic reports. Please refer to Table 9.2 for a summary and definition of these terms.

9.1.3   Terminology Associated with Skeletal Direction

When presenting the human skeleton in reports, the forensic anthropologist will describe the skeleton and its components in relation to the standard anatomical position (Figure 9.2). In standard anatomical position, the human skeleton, particularly the lower arm bones, are supinated or in the supine position (feet and the palms of the hands facing forward). In this position almost all the bones are visible, and none are crossed over one another.

Table 9.2 Descriptions of Features Associated with Bones That Are Commonly Used in Osteological Reports

Alveolus	A relatively large projection or prominent bump.
Articulation	The region where adjacent bones contact each other, usually forming a joint surface. To be truly articulated, bones must have soft tissue connecting them. Although some individuals may use the term *articulated* to describe an undisturbed skeleton, it is more correct to describe the skeleton as being in *anatomical position*.
Condyle	A large, rounded articular process.
Crest	A prominent ridge of bone that is commonly associated with muscle or ligament attachment.
Facet	A small, smooth articular surface.
Foramen	An opening or hole that goes through a bone.
Fossa	A broad, shallow depressed area.
Groove (Sulcus)	A deep or shallow trench on a bone that during life may contain a tendon or vessel.
Line (Ridge)	A long, thin projection of bone, often with a rough surface that is usually associated with muscle attachment.
Process	A projection of bone.
Sinus	A cavity or hollow area within a cranial bone.
Spine	A relatively long, thin projection or bump.
Suture	Articulation or joints between the cranial bones.
Trochanter	One of two specific tuberosities located on the femur.
Tubercle	A projection or bump with a roughened surface (usually associated with muscle attachment), generally smaller than a tuberosity.
Tuberosity	A projection or bump with a roughened surface (usually associated with muscle attachment).

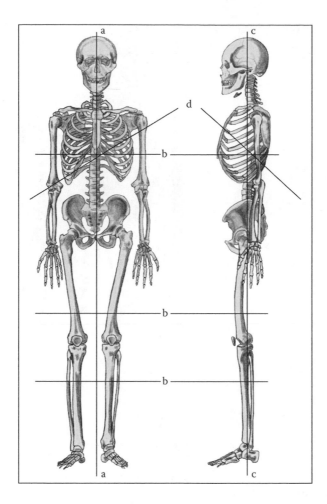

Figure 9.2   The human skeleton showing the standard anatomical position and anterior view (left), and lateral view (right). The planes of reference for the human skeleton are the (a) sagittal or medial plane, dividing the body into right and left halves; (b) transverse or horizontal plane, dividing the body into upper and lower sections at any level; (c) the frontal or coronal plane dividing the body into front and back halves; and (d) the oblique plane, which may transect the skeleton at any other angle.

If the lower arms are pronated or in the prone position (the palm of the hand facing backward), the radius is crossed over the ulna causing much of the ulna to be hidden. Most skeletal data recording sheets will include a drawing of a skeleton in the standard anatomical position, and this may be a common inclusion in medical examiner or forensic anthropologist reports (see Appendices 9 and 10). These drawings may be used to indicate the absence or presence of skeletal elements, or may also be used to illustrate pathology or trauma.

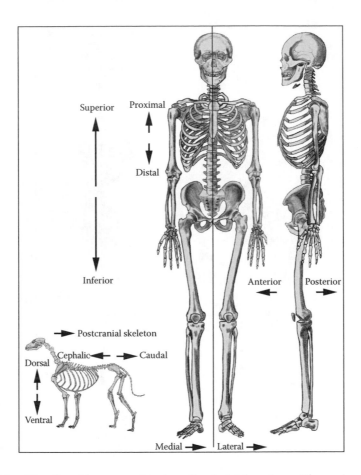

Figure 9.3   Directional terms used to describe skeletal anatomy. The canine skeleton (left) illustrates directional terms that are more suited for describing the quadrupedal skeleton. Those commonly used for the human skeleton are illustrated on the anterior (center) and lateral (right) views of the human skeleton.

The skeleton and independent skeletal elements may be referred to in reference to the anatomical planes (Figure 9.2). The sagittal or median plane divides the body down the center and creates a right and left half of the body. The coronal or frontal plane divides the body into front and back halves. The transverse or horizontal plane is used to divide the body at any level into superior and inferior parts. The oblique plane divides the body at any other angle.

There are several other directional terms that may appear in relation to the biological description of the skeleton, or even in the description of the skeleton as it appeared at the scene (Figure 9.3). The medical examiner or forensic anthropologist may use these terms to describe the location of taphonomic changes (such as carnivore chewing), pathology (such as healed fractures), or trauma (such as a gunshot wound or sharp-force trauma). These terms may also be used in field reports to describe the position of the skeleton or particular skeletal elements, or to describe the relationship between objects and the skeleton (for example, a bullet found beside the top of the humerus may be described as being located by the proximal or superior end of the humerus). The top or most superior end (toward the cranium) of a long bone is referred to as the proximal end of the bone, while its most inferior portion (toward the feet) is referred to as the distal end. Superior (also sometimes referred to as cephalic) and inferior (sometimes referred to as caudal) may also be used to describe portions of other bones in relation to where they lay in the skeleton. For example, the surface of the vertebra that is toward the cranium is the superior surface, while the bottom surface is inferior. The use of the descriptor terms cephalic (toward the brain) or caudal (toward the tail) are better used to describe quadrupedal skeletons, however some medical examiners may use this terminology for the human skeleton. Any part of the skeleton or bone that is found toward the middle of the body (or the midline) is referred to as medial, while any part of the body that is away from the midline is called lateral. Any portion of the skeleton or bone located toward the front of the body is described as anterior or ventral, while anything toward the back is described as posterior or dorsal.

The skeleton may also be divided into particular areas. The skull (cranium plus the mandible) is usually treated as one complex structure and is referred to as the cranial skeleton. While the investigator may come across the term postcranial to describe the entire skeleton located below the cranium, this term is more accurately used to describe the skeleton of a quadrupedal animal as it literally translates to "behind the cranium" (Figure 9.3). A more accurate term to describe the skeleton below the cranium for the bipedal human skeleton would be infracranial. The infracranial skeleton can also be divided into two further areas, the axial and the appendicular skeleton. The axial skeleton is found at the midline of the body and includes the spinal column, the ribs, the shoulder girdle, and the pelvis. The appendicular skeleton includes all the arm and leg bones. See Table 9.3 for a summary of all the directional terminology associated with the human skeleton.

9.2   Basic Adult Human Skeletal Biology

The average adult human skeleton contains 206 bones (see Figure 9.4). Take note, however, that there is human variation in the number of skeletal elements that each individual has, so there may be more or less than 206 bones, depending on genetics, development, and life history.

Table 9.3 Directional Terms Associated with the Description of the Human Skeleton

Standard anatomical position	Body faces forward, with palms facing forward so that all bones are visible (no bones are crossed over one another). Also referred to as the supine position.
Prone	Body position in which the palms of the hand are facing backwards, causing the radius to be crossed over the ulna.
Supine	Body position in which the palms of the hand are facing forward, causing the radius and ulna to be parallel to one another.
Sagittal (medial) plane	Plane of reference that divides the body into right and left halves.
Frontal (coronal) plane	Plane of reference that separates the body into front and back halves.
Transverse (horizontal) plane	Plane of reference that separates the body into upper and lower parts (can be found at any location along the body and is perpendicular to the sagittal and frontal planes).
Oblique plane	Plane of reference that is remove at any other angle on the body.
Superior	Toward the cranium (may also be referred to as cephalic). Used to describe bones of the axial skeleton.
Inferior	Away from the cranium (may also be referred to as caudal). Used to describe bones of the axial skeleton.
Proximal	End of the long bone closest to the axial portion of the body. Used to describe bones of the appendicular skeleton.
Distal	End of the long bone furthest away from the axial skeleton. Used to describe bones of the appendicular skeleton.
Medial	Toward the midline of the body.
Lateral	Away from the midline of the body.
Cranial skeleton	All the components of the skull (sometimes including the hyoid).
Infracranial skeleton	All the bones of the skeleton below the skull.
Axial skeleton	Bones of the thorax (including the shoulder girdle, ribs, vertebrae and pelvis).
Appendicular skeleton	All the bones of the limbs.

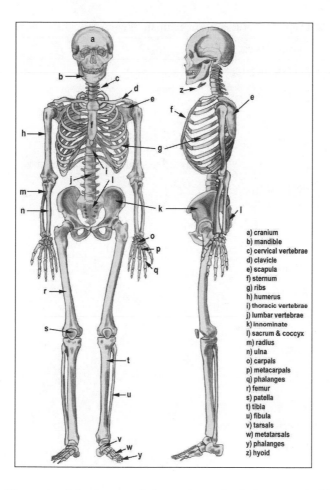

a) cranium
b) mandible
c) cervical vertebrae
d) clavicle
e) scapula
f) sternum
g) ribs
h) humerus
i) thoracic vertebrae
j) lumbar vertebrae
k) innominate
l) sacrum & coccyx
m) radius
n) ulna
o) carpals
p) metacarpals
q) phalanges
r) femur
s) patella
t) tibia
u) fibula
v) tarsals
w) metatarsals
y) phalanges
z) hyoid

Figure 9.4   Elements of the human skeleton shown in their anatomical location.

Table 9.4 contains an inventory of the adult human skeleton and Appendices 9 and 10 include inventory sheets that can be used for documentation of skeletal elements at the scene.

The adult skull (cranium plus mandible) contains an average of 29 bones when the hyoid is included. Please note that some anatomy textbooks include the hyoid (Figure 9.5) as part of the skull, while other texts include it as part of the axial skeleton (Byers, 2004). Although there are many situations in which the cranial bones will be separated (for example, if the skeleton has been exposed to high temperature fires, has experienced high impact blunt force trauma, or a gunshot wound), normally the majority of the cranial elements will be found in an articulated state. The exception to

Table 9.4 Inventory of the Adult Human Skeleton

Skull Bones			

BONES OF THE SKULL

Facial Bones (Splanchnocranium)

Mandible	1	Nasal	2
Vomer	1	Lacrimal	2
Maxilla	2	Palatine	2
Zygomatic	2	Inferior nasal concha	2

Cranial Vault Bones (Calvarium)

Frontal	1	Sphenoid	1	
Occipital	1	Temporal	2	
Ethmoid	1	Parietal	2	
Auditory ossicles	6	Hyoid	1	
Total Skull Bones				29

BONES OF THE INFRACRANIAL SKELETON

Axial Skeleton

Cervical vertebra	7	Coccyx (4-5 fused)	1	
Thoracic vertebra	12	Sternum	1	
Lumbar vertebra	5	Ribs	24	
Sacrum	1	Clavicle	2	
Innominate	2	Scapula	2	
Total Axial Bones				57

Appendicular Skeleton

Humerus	2	Carpals	16	
Ulna	2	Metacarpals	10	
Radius	2	Hand phalanges	28	
Femur	2	Tarsals	14	
Tibia	2	Metatarsals	10	
Fibula	2	Foot phalanges	28	
Patella	2			
Total Appendicular Bones				120
TOTAL BONES IN THE ADULT SKELETON				206

this would be the mandible, the hyoid, and the ear ossicles, all of which are not secured to the cranium in the event that the soft tissue decomposes. Figure 9.6 shows the skull in four views so that all the different bones can be identified. It is useful to be familiar with the different bones of the skull as both medical examiners and forensic anthropologists will refer to the separate

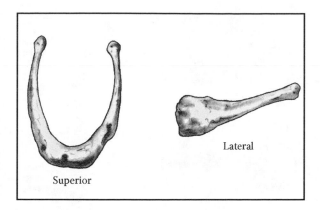

Figure 9.5 Superior and lateral views of the hyoid bone (located under the mandible, see Figure 9.4).

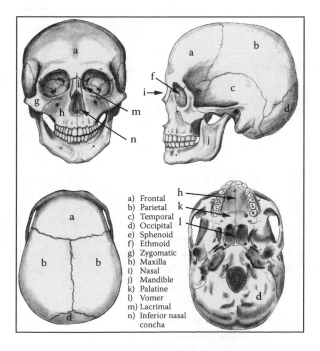

a) Frontal
b) Parietal
c) Temporal
d) Occipital
e) Sphenoid
f) Ethmoid
g) Zygomatic
h) Maxilla
i) Nasal
j) Mandible
k) Palatine
l) Vomer
m) Lacrimal
n) Inferior nasal concha

Figure 9.6 Bones of the skull presented on the anterior view (upper left), lateral view (upper right), superior view (lower left) and inferior view (lower right).

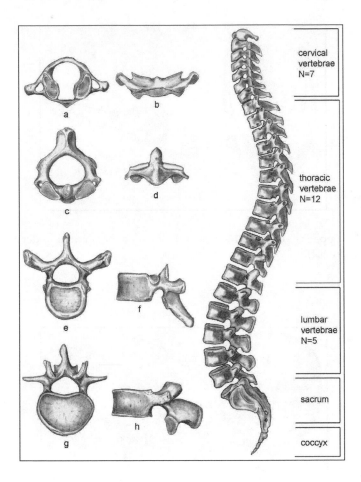

Figure 9.7   Vertebral column of the human skeleton. The far right shows an articulated spine with the number of segments that are assigned to each vertebral category. The individual vertebra illustrate some of the differences between vertebral types: (a) superior view of the first cervical vertebra (C1), also known as the atlas; (b) anterior view of C1; (c) superior view of C2, also known as the axis; (d) anterior view of C2; (e) superior view of thoracic vertebra #6 (T6); (f) lateral view of T6; (g) superior view of lumbar vertebra #2 (L2); (h) lateral view of L2.

bones of the skull when documenting the location of pathology or trauma. See Table 9.4 for a list of the bones of the skull.

The axial skeleton is composed of 57 bones that include the vertebral column (Figure 9.7), the ribs and sternum (Figure 9.8), the shoulder girdle (Figure 9.9), and the pelvis (Figure 9.10). The thorax area, which comprises most of the axial skeleton, is an area of the body that is most likely to bear evidence of sharp force trauma (for example, stab wounds), and therefore it

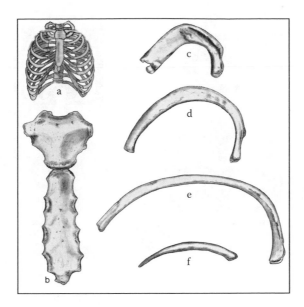

Figure 9.8 The articulated thorax (a), composed of the sternum (b), ribs (c-f), and vertebral column (shown in Figure 9.7). The ribs can be distinguished by their morphology: superior surface of rib #1 (c); superior surface of rib #2 (d); superior surface of rib #8 (e); and the superior surface of rib #12 (f).

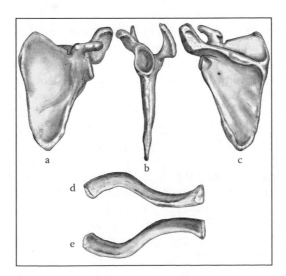

Figure 9.9 Bones of the shoulder girdle. The left scapula is shown in (a) the anterior view; (b) lateral view; and (c) the posterior view. The inferior surface of the left clavicle is shown in (d), and the superior surface is shown in (e).

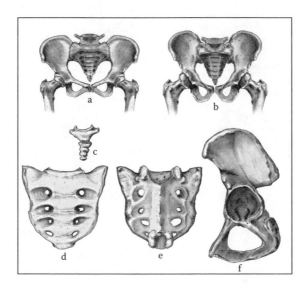

Figure 9.10   The bones of the pelvic girdle: (a) and (b) show the articulated pelvis of an adult female (a) and male (b). The coccyx vertebrae are shown in (c) while the anterior surface of the sacrum is shown in (d) and the posterior surface is shown in (e). The lateral view of a single left pelvic bone is shown in (f).

is important that all bones be collected from the scene if possible. We have presented illustrations for both the articulated parts of the axial skeleton and singular bones, since it is just as likely to find single scattered bones since it is to find a skeleton in anatomical position in a forensic case.

The appendicular skeleton comprises both the arm and leg bones for a total of 120 bones. The bones of the arm (shown articulated and singularly in Figure 9.11) consist of the humerus, the ulna, and the radius. The hand is made up of eight carpals, five metacarpals, five proximal phalanges, four intermediate phalanges (the first phalange, or thumb, does not have an intermediate phalange), and five distal phalanges (Figure 9.12). The bones of the leg (shown articulated and in singular in Figure 9.13) consist of the femur, the patella, the tibia, and the fibula. Each foot consists of seven tarsals, five metatarsals, five proximal phalanges, four intermediate phalanges (the first phalange, or big toe, does not have an intermediate phalange), and five distal phalanges (Figure 9.14). Although the hand and foot bones are small, it is very important that they are recognized and collected from a scene. Forensically relevant information such as defense wounds to the hands may be present on these small bones and may be vital for reconstructing the events surrounding an individual's death. See Table 9.5 for a list of the separate hand and foot bones.

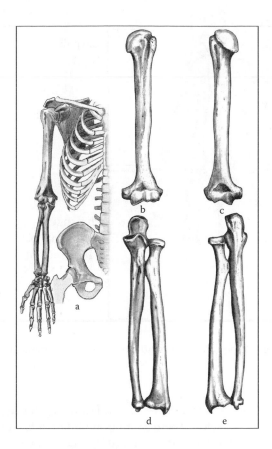

Figure 9.11 Bones of the arm and hand are shown articulated in (a); (b) and (c) show the anterior and posterior views of the left humerus; (d) shows the anterior view of the left articulated ulna (on the left or medial side) and radius (on the right or lateral); (e) shows the posterior view of the left articulated ulna (on the right) and radius (on the left).

9.3   The Subadult Skeleton

It should be noted that the fetal, infant, child, and teenage or adolescent skeleton has a different morphological appearance and can contain far more bones than the adult skeleton (see Appendix 11 for an inventory drawing of the juvenile skeleton). At eleven weeks before birth there are usually about 800 bony pieces of the skeleton and at birth there are about 450. There are several small bony elements called epiphyses that will eventually fuse to the shafts of the long bones and other skeletal elements. As an individual grows, more skeletal elements will appear and eventually all these elements will fuse together to form the adult skeleton. By adulthood, normally between the ages of 21 to 25, all of the epiphyses (see section 9.1.1) have fused and 206 bones remain in the body (White, 2000).

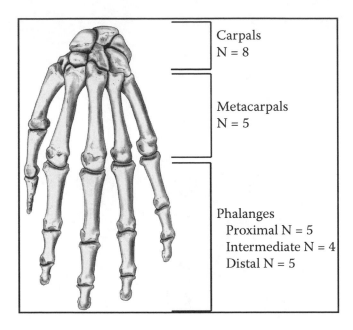

Carpals
N = 8

Metacarpals
N = 5

Phalanges
  Proximal N = 5
  Intermediate N = 4
  Distal N = 5

Figure 9.12   Bones of the wrist and hand presented in anatomical position.

Refer to Figure 9.15 for an example of how a femur (upper leg bone) changes during growth of the skeleton. These small bone fragments can be easily overlooked or misidentified at the crime scene (they may appear as small rocks or twigs), but can be of vital importance for the identification of the individual.

An infant or fetal skeleton (Figure 9.16) looks considerably different than an adult skeleton. Bones of the skeleton are commonly light brown in color, and may appear to the untrained eye as small twigs, debris, or be mistaken as the skeleton of a nonhuman animal. As a result, they are easily missed at the scene. Occasionally, it may be necessary to identify fetal bones in a field situation if a female victim was pregnant, or in the case that a fetus or infant is part of a scene. Although it may seem like this would be a rarity, the authors have participated in forensic cases in which the identification and estimation of fetal age greatly assisted in the identification of the victim. Care should be taken when removing dirt and debris from the pelvic area of any human skeleton, as this would be the most likely location of fetal remains, if they were present.

9.4 Human Dentition

Humans typically have two sets of teeth, the deciduous, also called the primary, baby, or milk teeth, and the permanent, also called the secondary or adult teeth. Teeth can be a very important part of a forensic investigation as positive identification of the individual can be made with comparisons to dental records. The dentition is the only part of the human skeleton that

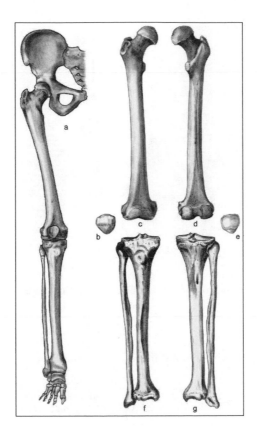

Figure 9.13 Bones of the leg are shown articulated in (a); (b) and (e) show the anterior and posterior views of the patella; (c) and (d) show the anterior and posterior views of the right femur; (f) shows the anterior view of the right articulated tibia (on the left or medial side) and fibula (on the right or lateral); (g) shows the posterior view of the left articulated tibia (on the right) and fibula (on the left).

comes into regular contact with the environment during a person's life. For that reason they can retain modifications that occur during the life of the individual, be it intentional or unintentional. For example, trips to the dentist may alter the teeth (for example, fillings, tooth extraction, root canals) in a way that can be used to identify the person after death.

9.4.1 Terminology Associated with the Human Dentition

When describing the dentition, the teeth are divided into four quadrants by running a line through the midline of the mouth at the sagittal plane (i.e., left and right), and another that divides the mouth into an upper and lower half (i.e., the maxilla and the mandible) (Figure 9.17). This creates upper right, upper left, lower right, and lower left quadrants. The deciduous dentition

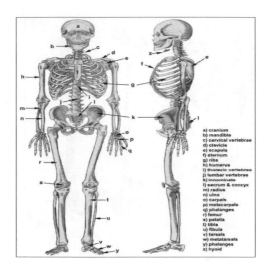

Figure 9.14   Bones of the foot shown in anatomical position.

Table 9.5 List of the Bones Found in the Hands and Feet

Hand (N=27)	Foot (N=26)
Carpals (wrist bones; N=8)	Tarsals (ankle bones; N=7)
Lunate	Calcaneus
Scaphoid	Talus
Triquetral	Navicular
Pisiform	Cuboid
Trapezium	1st Cuneiform
Trapezoid	2nd Cuneiform
Capitate	3rd Cuneiform
Hamate	
Metacarpals (bones of the palm of the hand) N=5	Metatarsals (bones of the arch of the foot) N=5
Metacarpal 1	Metatarsal 1
Metacarpal 2	Metatarsal 2
Metacarpal 3	Metatarsal 3
Metacarpal 4	Metatarsal 4
Metacarpal 5	Metatarsal 5
Phalanges (finger bones)	Phalanges (toe bones)
Proximal (N=5)	Proximal (N=5)
Intermediate (N=4)	Intermediate (N=4)
Distal (N=5)	Distal (N=5)

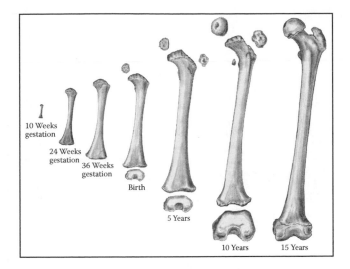

Figure 9.15 Anterior view of the growth stages of the left femur, illustrating the appearance of epiphyses and the growth of the diaphysis at different stages of development.

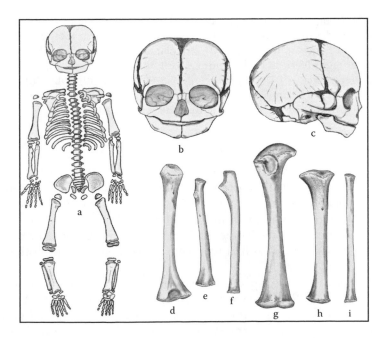

Figure 9.16 Bones of the fetal skeleton: (a) shows the articulated fetal skeleton, and demonstrates that there are many more skeletal elements at this stage of development. The skull is also in many pieces as shown in (b) anterior view of the fetal skull, and (c) lateral view of the fetal skull. The long bones of the fetal skeleton are shown in (d) the humerus, (e) the radius, (f) the ulna, (g) the femur, (h) the tibia, and (i) the fibula.

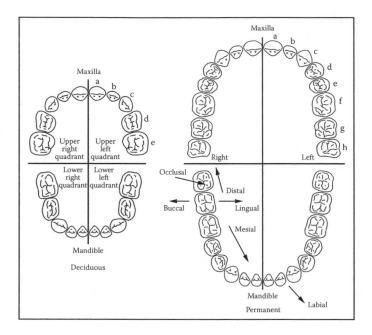

Figure 9.17   Comparison of the deciduous (left) and permanent dentition (right). The deciduous dentition has five teeth in each quadrant for a total of 20 teeth: (a) 1st incisor, (b) 2nd incisor, (c) canine, (d) 1st molar, and (e) 2nd molar. The permanent dentition has eight teeth in each quadrant for a total of 32 teeth: (a) 1st incisor, (b) 2nd incisor, (c) canine, (d) 1st premolar, (e) 2nd premolar, (f) 1st molar, (g) 2nd molar, and (h) 3rd molar. The image of the permanent dentition (right) also shows the directional terms associated with the surfaces of a single tooth.

is made up of five different teeth in each of the four dental quadrants for a total of 20 teeth. In each quadrant there are two incisors, one canine, and two baby molars. The permanent dentition is made up of eight tooth types in each of the four dental quadrants for a total of 32 teeth. In each quadrant there are two incisors, one canine, two premolars, and three molars. During middle childhood an individual will have mixed dentition, or both deciduous and permanent teeth.

Each tooth is made up of a crown, root, pulp cavity, and an apical foramen (Figure 9.18). The structural components of the tooth include the enamel, dentin, and cementum. The point at which the enamel ends and the cementum begins is referred to as the cemento-enamel junction, or the CEJ. During life, the tooth is held into the tooth socket by the periodontal ligament.

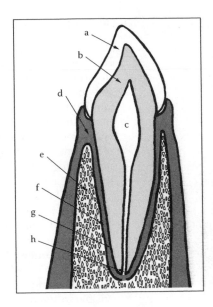

Figure 9.18 Cross-section of a lower incisor showing the components of a tooth: (a) enamel, (b) dentin, (c) pulp cavity, (d) gingiva, (e) bone, (f) periodontal ligament, (g) cementum, and (h) apical canal.

As with the skeleton, there are directional and descriptor terms that are used by the dentist, medical examiner, and forensic anthropologist to describe teeth and any remarkable modification of them. Each tooth has six directional planes that are commonly used to describe the location of modifications such as cavities or fillings (Figure 9.17). The chewing surface of the tooth is called the occlusal surface (this may be called the incisal surface on incisors). The surface of premolars and molars facing the anterior of the mouth and the surface of the canines and incisors facing the midline of the mouth is called the mesial surface, while the opposite surface is called the distal surface The surface of the tooth facing the tongue is called the lingual surface, while the opposite side on molars and premolars is referred to as the buccal surface, and on the canines and incisors is called the labial surface. The surface or direction toward the tip of the root is referred to as the apical surface. Refer to Table 9.6 for a summary of all the terms associated with the dentition.

9.4.2 Dental Numbering Systems

Worldwide there are many different systems that dentists use to assign identity to each tooth. Here we present the two most widely used systems so that investigators can interpret which teeth are being discussed in a

Table 9.6 Terminology Associated with the Dentition That May Appear in Forensic Reports

Enamel	The hard, white mineral portion of the tooth that makes up the majority of the tooth crown.
Dentin	Internal tissue in a tooth crown and root, surrounding the pulp cavity and surrounded by the crown enamel. This bone-like substance is softer than the enamel.
Cementum	The tissue covering tooth roots that anchors them to the periodontal ligament.
Cemento-enamel junction (CEJ)	The point at which the enamel ends and the cementum begins.
Pulp chamber	The inner portion of the tooth that contains the blood and nerve supply.
Crown	Upper portion of the tooth that is visible in the mouth.
Cusp	A small elevation on the occlusal surface of a tooth (primarily found on the premolars and molars).
Root	The portion of a tooth that is embedded in the jaw and serves as support.
Periodontal ligament	Soft tissue ligament that holds the tooth into the tooth socket.
Occlusal	Chewing surfaces of all the teeth.
Incisal	Chewing surface of the incisors.
Buccal	Surface of the molars and premolars that face the cheek.
Labial	Surface of the incisors and canines that face the lips.
Lingual	Surface of the tooth that faces the tongue.
Apical	Toward the tip of the root of the tooth.
Mesial	Toward the anterior or midline of the mouth.
Distal	Opposite of mesial, toward the back of the mouth.

report (for example, if a forensic odontologist uses the dentition to make a positive identification, they will commonly discuss singular teeth used to make the match, and these teeth will be referred to according to a dental numbering system). In North America, the standard used by dentists to

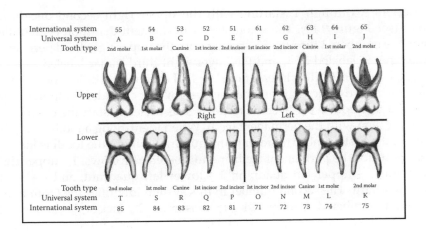

Figure 9.19 Identification of each tooth in the deciduous dentition. The Universal and International tooth numbering systems are shown for each tooth.

number teeth is called the Universal or National dental numbering system. The other most accepted system worldwide is called the International system or the FDI system.

In the Universal system, dentists use a simple number or letter to identify each tooth. The primary or deciduous dentition is identified using

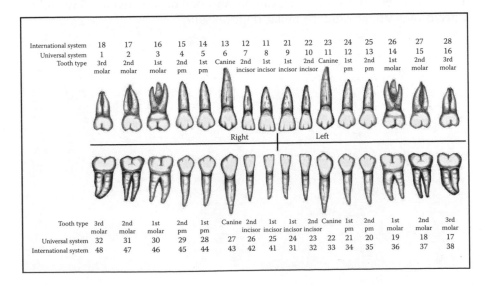

Figure 9.20 Identification of each tooth in the permanent dentition. The Universal and International tooth numbering systems are shown for each tooth.

the letters A through T, starting with the upper right second deciduous molar (see Figure 9.19). The secondary or permanent dentition is identified using the numbers 1 through 32, starting with the upper right third permanent molar that is labeled as 1, and the lower right third molar labeled as tooth 32 (see Figure 9.20). The International or FDI system is a little more complicated, using a double-digit numbering system that considers both the quadrant and the tooth type. In some respects, it is easier to start the description of this system with the permanent teeth. When identifying a tooth using this system, the first number represents the quadrant where the tooth is located. Quadrants for the permanent teeth are numbered as follows: 1 – upper right quadrant; 2 – upper left quadrant; 3 – lower left quadrant; and 4 – lower right quadrant. The second number in this system identifies the tooth types, which are numbered as follows: 1 – 1st incisor; 2 – 2nd incisor; 3- canine; 4- 1st premolar; 5 – 2nd premolar; 6 – 1st molar; 7 – 2nd molar; and 8 – 3rd premolar. Thus, a tooth labeled as 36 would be a permanent lower left 1st molar, and a tooth labeled as 14 would represent a permanent upper right 1st premolar (Figure 9.20). The deciduous dentition follows a similar pattern, with the first number identifying the quadrant, and the second number identifying the tooth type. The quadrant designations for the deciduous teeth are a continuation of the permanent dentition, and are numbered as follows: 5 – upper right quadrant; 6 – upper left quadrant; 7 – lower left quadrant; and 8 – lower right quadrant. Since there are only five tooth types in each of the deciduous quadrants they are numbered as: 1 – 1st incisor; 2 – 2nd incisor; 3 – canine; 4 – 1st molar; and 5 – 2nd molar. Therefore, a tooth labeled 73 would represent a deciduous lower left canine, and one designated as 55 would be a deciduous upper right 2nd molar (Figure 9.19).

chapter 10

Distinguishing Nonhuman Skeletal Remains

Distinguishing between human and nonhuman bone is a task that should only be undertaken by a forensic anthropologist or individuals experienced in osteology. The purpose of including this chapter is twofold — first, it is included to demonstrate that nonhuman bones can easily be mistaken for human bones and to reinforce why an experienced osteologist should be making the final determination; and second, this chapter is also included for forensic anthropology students to introduce them to different examples of nonhuman bones that can be easily confused with human bones. There are several questions that the experienced forensic anthropologist or forensic archaeologist should be able to answer in the field. These include determining whether the suspected material is actually bone, and if it is bone, is it human or nonhuman? For example, rocks will appear in shapes that can mimic human bones. One rule of thumb is that rocks are usually heavier than bone. The irregular bones that could be mistaken for rocks such as the patella, carpals (wrist bones), or tarsals (ankle bones) tend to have a higher concentration of trabecular or cancellous bone, making them significantly lighter than rocks. An experienced forensic anthropologist will have no problem distinguishing nonosseous material from bone.

More commonly, the forensic anthropologist will be asked to determine whether the skeletal material is human or nonhuman. In many cases, being able to differentiate human from faunal bones enables the investigator to eliminate what may have been at first considered to be a forensic case (although, some nonhuman remains may be forensically relevant). William Bass (1995), a noted forensic anthropologist, has stated that as many as 25 to 30% of all the cases submitted to forensic anthropologists for identification are nonhuman in nature and many of those end up being butchered domestic animals (Figure 10.1). Thus, basic knowledge of the human skeleton and nonhuman skeleton can help to save time when determining the forensic significance of whole or fragmentary skeletal remains. Of course, as a rule of thumb, all bones recovered from a scene should be examined by a forensic

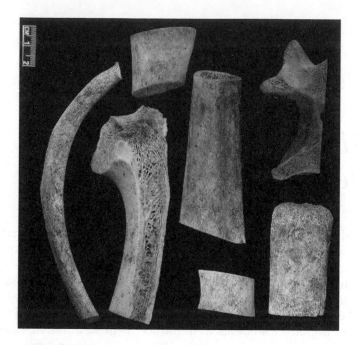

Figure 10.1　Examples of butchered nonhuman remains. Note the sharp edges, which are indicative of saw marks or deliberate dismemberment.

anthropologist, since such an expert will have the expertise to determine whether the bones are human or nonhuman. If you do not have a forensic anthropologist on the scene or readily available, one suggestion is to take digital photographs and email them to a forensic anthropologist. Many forensic anthropologists have reviewed photos via email to make the determination of human versus nonhuman bones. This can save a tremendous amount of time and resources.

It is important for trained osteologists to be familiar with animals that are located in their geographical region when considering the species that might be confused with human bones. Osteologists can become familiar with nonhuman animal bones by putting together a comparative collection of local bones from known species. They can then use this collection to determine the species of questionable bones. In addition to having a comparative collection, or in a case in which a comparative collection is not available, there are various books that can be consulted for a more in-depth consideration of nonhuman skeletal biology. For guides to mammalian osteology, we suggest *Mammalian Osteology* by B.M. Gilbert (1990), *Mammal Bones and Teeth: An Introductory Guide to Methods of Identification* by S. Hillson (1992), and *Mammal Remains from Archaeological Sites* by S.J. Olsen (1996). For more information about bird skeletal structure we recommend the *Manual of Ornithology: Avian Structure and Function* by N.S. Proctor and P.J. Lynch (1993).

10.1 Distinguishing Humans from Other Mammals

Large mammal bones such as bear, deer, large dogs, and pigs are most often confused with adult human bones, and small animals may be confused with juvenile or fetal bones. In particular, when bones are highly weathered, eroded, and fragmented, identification may only be possible when conducted by a trained osteologist. From an anatomical perspective, humans and other non-human mammals can be very similar in their skeletal components, and because humans are mammals, they possess many of the same skeletal characteristics. For example, the number and types of bones are similar among mammals. In addition, key features, such as bone structure, are similar so that most mammals have long bone shafts that are composed of thick cortical bone and long bone ends that are composed of trabecular bone. In fact, if just a small bone fragment is recovered without any morphological indicators, the only way to identify whether it is human or nonhuman would be through histological (microscopic) examination or DNA analysis.

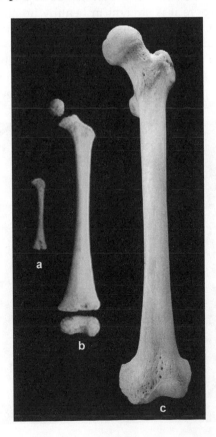

Figure 10.2 Comparison of different stages of growth of a human femur. This view shows (a) the anterior left femora, from a newborn without epiphyses; (b) a child of approximately 3 years of age with epiphyses; and (c) an adult who has completed growth.

Upon gross examination, there are two main characteristics of bones that can help make the distinction between human and nonhuman bone easy and expeditious: maturity and morphology. Maturity aids in differentiating small nonhuman animals that, even after reaching adulthood, have bones that are similar in size when compared with juvenile humans. As discussed in Chapter 9, depending on the level of development, juvenile human long bones may have unfused separate epiphyses or may not possess any at all (Figure 10.2). Conversely, those of a small adult nonhuman animal will display fused epiphyses. As a result, nonhuman bones can be easily differentiated from juvenile humans by examining the level of bone maturity (Figure 10.3). The proximal and distal ends of the juvenile long bones are roughened in appearance where the epiphyses will eventually fuse to the metaphysis. In addition, other morphological indicators that can be useful when differentiating small animals from human juvenile long bones may include nonhuman skeletal features such as the fusion of fibula and tibia, and the curvature of the long bone shaft (diaphysis). For example, the long bone shaft of small mammals may be noticeably curved where it is straight in healthy juveniles (Figure 10.4). An example of the characteristics that distinguish juvenile human long bones from those of small adult animals is illustrated in Figure 10.5

One structure of small mammals that could possibly be confused with human or fetal bones is the pelvis. If a small pelvis is fused into one unit, it will be a nonhuman pelvis because a human juvenile pelvis of a comparable

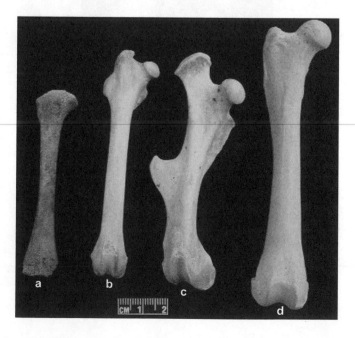

Figure 10.3   Pictorial comparison of the anterior view of (a) a right newborn femur, with those of small adult mammals such as a (b) rabbit; (c) an armadillo; and (d) a raccoon.

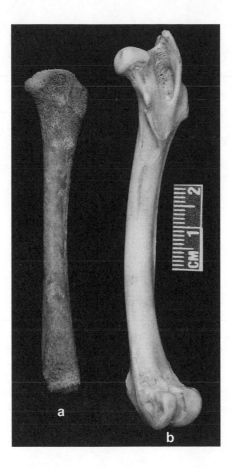

Figure 10.4 Difference in diaphyseal curvature (shown in lateral view) between (a) a human newborn femur and (b) a raccoon.

size is still in multiple pieces (Figure 10.6) and the two adult pelvic bones of the human do not fuse at all unless there is a pathological condition.

The second characteristic of bone that aids in the distinction between human and nonhuman mammalian bone is morphology, or the shape of the bone. As mentioned previously, humans and other mammals share the same kinds of bones (for example, two femora, two humeri, two scapulae) and we share the same basic architecture required by our soft tissue structures. Because humans are bipedal they have distinct morphological features related to walking upright, which distinguish them from all quadrupeds that are adapted for four-legged locomotion. Figure 10.7 presents two examples of the generalized mammalian skeleton, to illustrate some of the skeletal features that are related to quadrupedal locomotion in a dog and bison. When comparing humans and other mammals, the dissimilarity in the shape of long bones and other bones of the body such as the

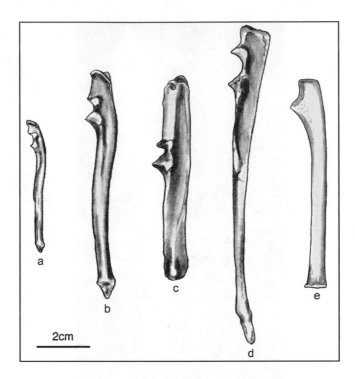

Figure 10.5   Comparison of (e) an anterior right human fetal/infant ulna to ulnae from small mature nonhuman animals. Posterior/lateral view of left radii from (a) a squirrel; (b) opossum; (c) armadillo; and (d) a fox.

scapula (Figure 10.8) can be very distinct and can quickly lead to a positive identification of human or nonhuman remains. For example, in a number of small animals, including mammals, the fibula is reduced in size and is fused to the shaft of the tibia (Figure 10.9). In humans, the fibula does not normally fuse to the tibia unless there is pathology such as ossification of ligaments that serve to keep both bones articulated together. Furthermore, some larger mammal species (e.g., pig, sheep, and deer) also have a curved and fused radius and ulna (Figure 10.10). Recognition of these two bones immediately excludes humans as both the radius and ulna have straight diaphysis, and remain unfused throughout life. See Figures 10.11 and 10.12 to illustrate the morphological differences between the adult human and additional nonhuman long bones.

Mammals belonging to the order artiodactyl (hoofed mammals that have an even number of toes on each foot — two or four) can be easily distinguished from humans by the presence of metapodials. In these animals (for example, deer, sheep, goat, moose, caribou), the third and fourth metacarpals and metatarsals are fused together into one structure early in development, and the generic name for both is metapodial.

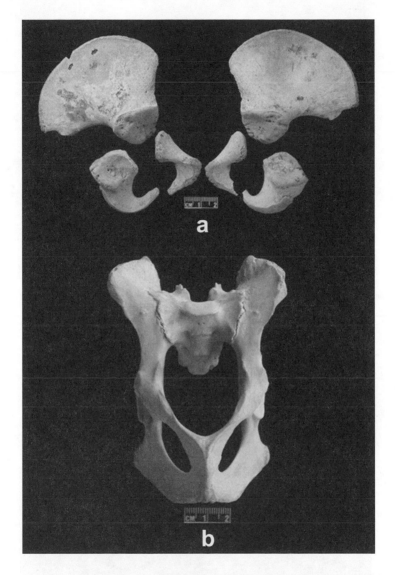

Figure 10.6   Comparison between (a) a human child pelvis and that of (b) an adult raccoon. Although roughly the same size, the human pelvis remains unfused in young children, and the sacrum always remains as a separate unit.

Metapodials are long in certain species and therefore could be easily mistaken as long bones. Metapodials are easily recognized by a number of morphological indicators (Figure 10.13) — the shafts are long, thin, and straight, and they still retain a clear groove down the shaft where they have fused; the proximal articulation is flat; and the distal articulation is unique with double rounded articulations. Furthermore, metacarpals and metatarsals can be

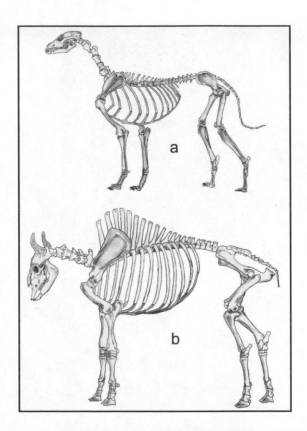

Figure 10.7   Quadrupedal mammalian skeletons (canid: top; bison: bottom).

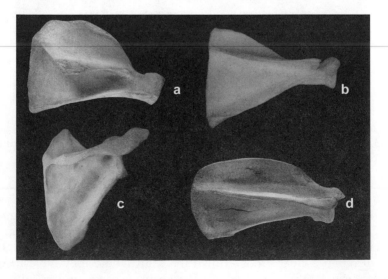

Figure 10.8   Comparison of mammalian scapulae: (a) pig; (b) sheep; (c) adult human; and (d) dog. (Not to scale.)

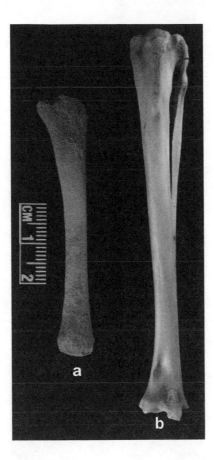

Figure 10.9 Comparison between (a) a human newborn tibia and (b) the fused tibia and fibula of the rabbit.

distinguished from one another by the cross-sectional shape of their shaft — metatarsals are square-shaped and metacarpals are D-shaped in cross section.

The human cranium is quite distinct from any other mammal because humans have a large, rounded braincase and flat, or orthognathic, face in profile. Because human crania are so distinct from other mammals, and misdiagnosis is unlikely, further differentiation will not be discussed.

10.2 The Bird Skeleton

There are several differences between a bird and human skeleton. Of course, birds have a very distinctive cranium, being the one and only animal to have a beak. Overall, birds tend to have fewer bones than mammals (Figure 10.14), and almost all bird skeletons are light in weight because they are adapted

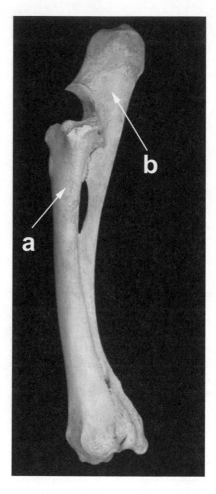

Figure 10.10   Curved diaphyses and fusion of the (a) radius and (b) ulna in a sheep.

for flight. Such adaptations include the presence of the furculum (also known as the wishbone), and the synsacrum, which is the large number of fused vertebrae that form a solid skeletal connection between the axial skeleton, the vertebra and the pelvic girdle. Another distinct feature is that the bodies of the vertebrae are saddle-shaped. The sternum on many birds, but not all, has a feature called the carina, a keel-like structure to which the muscles for flight are attached. The forelimb of a bird is fused so there is a reduction in the number of bones located in the carpal, metacarpal, and phalangeal regions in comparison with mammals. In addition, the bird skeleton is also unique because the lower limb is comprised of three long bone segments (Figure 10.14). The most proximal is the femur, followed by the union of the proximal part of the tarsus with the tibia, and the distal

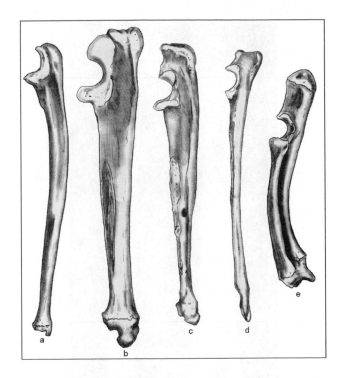

Figure 10.11   Comparison of mammalian ulnae (anterior view): (a) human; (b) black bear; (c) mountain lion; (d) coyote; and (e) pig (ulna and radius fused together). (Not to scale.)

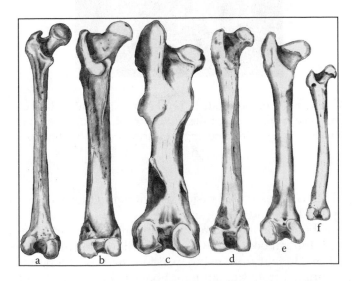

Figure 10.12   Comparison of mammalian femora (posterior view): (a) human; (b) black bear; (c) horse; (d) mountain lion; (e) deer; and (f) coyote. (Not to scale.)

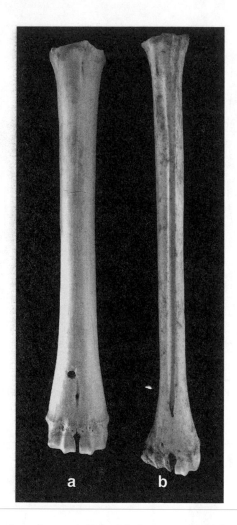

Figure 10.13   Examples of metapodials: (a) sheep metatarsal and (b) deer metacarpal. The larger hole located toward the distal end of the (a) sheep metatarsal was
drilled postmortem to assist in removing fat during the maceration process.

segment, which is the extended fusion of foot bones that give extra leverage
for running, landing, and taking off.

The long bones of large birds (for example, a stork's leg) may be
confused with human bones, however, the unique morphology of the bird
bone should preclude it from being misidentified. Bird long bones can be
easily differentiated from human long bones because they are lighter and
have an outer surface that is generally smooth except for the ends, which
contain articulation surfaces and small muscle attachment sites (Figure 10.15).
Another special feature of the bird long bone is the actual structure of the bone.

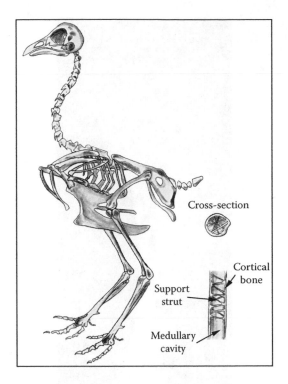

Figure 10.14 Complete articulated turkey skeleton, with cross-section of femur shown at right.

What makes a bird skeleton light is that its long bones have thin cortical bone and are hollow. Within long bones are small spicules, or struts of bone, that cross the medullary cavity, giving the bone structural support (Figure 10.14) like that of an airplane wing. This feature is unique to birds and is not found in any other animal.

10.3 The Reptilian Skeleton

Reptiles include animals such as turtles, lizards, snakes, and alligators. Reptiles have many unique skeletal characteristics that make them readily identifiable (Figure 10.16). Reptiles possess a ball and socket type joint articulation between their vertebrae, with the cranial side of the vertebra being concave, and the caudal side being convex (Figure 10.17). The lower jaw of a reptile consists of several bones. In addition, reptile jaws have peg-like teeth (Figure 10.18) that are all the same type (referred to as homodont dentition). This is related to their feeding, as reptiles do not chew their food; instead they bite, tear, and swallow.

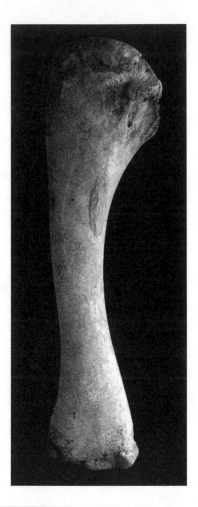

Figure 10.15   Turkey humerus with a very smooth cortical surface, lacking prominent muscle attachments.

A number of morphological indicators of reptile long bones can be useful when differentiating them from human long bones. In particular, alligator bones could cause some confusion in comparison with humans, as alligator bones can be large. However, alligator long bones should be easily differentiated from human long bones. Overall, reptile long bones can be classified as being moderately heavy in comparison with other animals, and they are not transparent. Reptile long bones have thick cortical bone, a very small medullary cavity, and do not have epiphyses. In addition, reptile bones such as those from an alligator do not have the roughened and prominent muscle attachment sites that are on human bones (Figure 10.19).

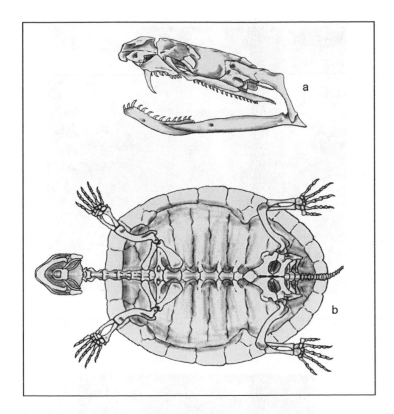

Figure 10.16   Representations of reptilian skeletons: (a) cobra skull and (b) turtle.

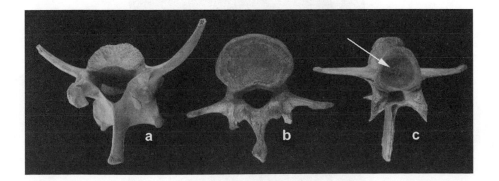

Figure 10.17   Alligator vertebrae (c) can be confused with vertebrae from other large mammals such as (a) deer and (b) humans . Alligator vertebra can be identified by the concave and convex surfaces on the vertebral bodies compared with flat body surfaces on mammals. The concave inferior surface of the alligator vertebra in this image is indicated by an arrow.

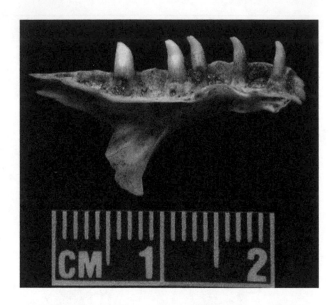

Figure 10.18   An example of homodont reptilian dentition from a lizard.

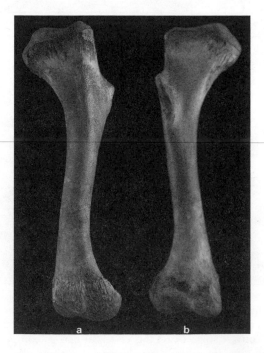

Figure 10.19   Anterior (a) and posterior (b) views of an alligator femur showing the smooth cortical surface, lack of prominent muscle attachments, and lack of defined epiphyses.

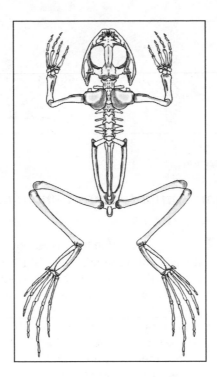

Figure 10.20   Amphibian (frog) skeleton.

10.4   The Amphibian Skeleton

Amphibians include animals such as frogs, toads, and salamanders. Their bones are very light and few in number (Figure 10.20). There is great diversity among amphibious species as to the thickness of the cortical bone, and whether or not their long bones have medullary cavities. One consistent feature is that amphibian bones do not have epiphyses. Some species have cartilaginous ends to their bones, and once decomposed the bones can exist as hollow tubes. For the most part, there should not be any confusion between amphibian and human bone as amphibians are usually small, and possess very unique skeletal morphology.

10.5   The Fish Skeleton

There should be no confusion identifying fish bones, because their morphology is very different from any other animal. In comparison with the mammalian skeleton, fish have fewer bones (Figure 10.21), and as they are adapted to an aquatic environment, all of the bones reflect an adaptation for swimming. The bony elements of fish skeletons do not have cancellous bone, nor do they have medullary spaces. They do not have epiphyses, and they are commonly described as being transparent or semitransparent.

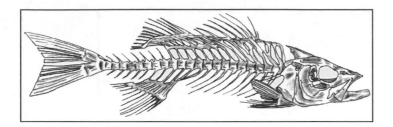

Figure 10.21   Fish skeleton.

10.6 *Nonhuman Animal Bones Commonly Confused with Human Bones*

There are several nonhuman animals that have bone structures or features that appear similar to human skeletal material. Table 10.1 presents a summary of some of the skeletal features that may be used to distinguish the different classes of animals. There are some bones, however, that are more commonly misidentified. Animal bones that might be confused include the bones of a bear paw, pig teeth, the knee of a pig, and a turtle shell. Disarticulated bear paws are commonly confused with human hands (Figure 10.22). After a hunted bear has been killed, the claws are usually removed as a trophy and the paws are sometimes discarded after they are skinned. There is a striking resemblance between a bear paw and a human hand after decomposition of the soft tissue has started. The bear paw can be easily identified by examining the individual bones, and it can also be easily differentiated from a human hand without cleaning the soft tissue from the bone. A radiograph can be

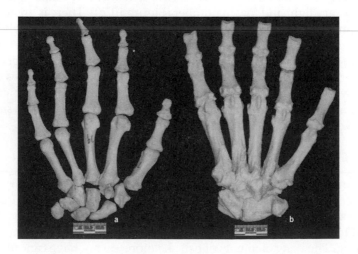

Figure 10.22   Human hand bones (a) compared with those of a bear (b).

Table 10.1 Comparison of Structural and Morphological Skeletal Differences between Human and Nonhuman Animals That May Potentially Be Found in a Forensic Context

Animal	Relative Weight	Transparency	Bone Surface Morphology	Cortical Bone	Medullary Cavity	Epiphyses
Humans	Heavy	Not transparent	Well developed	Thick	Small	Distinguished
Mammals	Heavy	Not transparent	Well developed	Thick	Small	Distinguished
Birds	Light	Not transparent	Well developed	Thin	Large	Some species
Fish	Light	Transparent or semi-transparent	Moderately developed	Noncancellous	Absent	Absent
Amphibians	Light	Not transparent	Poorly developed	Varies	Varies	Absent
Reptiles	Moderately heavy	Not transparent	Almost absent	Moderately thick	Reduced or absent	Varies

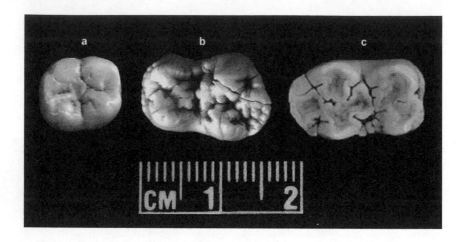

Figure 10.23   Comparison of a (a) human lower molar with that of (b) an unworn pig molar, and (c) a worn pig molar.

used to differentiate the bear paw from the human hand because the morphology of human hand bones is clearly different.

Pig molar teeth also show a striking resemblance to human molars because pigs are omnivorous like humans and their teeth are designed for a generalized diet (Figure 10.23). However, pig molars are larger than human molars and have pointier cusps. In addition, the proximal part of the pig tibia, called the tibial plateau, can be easily misidentified as a human tibial plateau by an inexperienced osteologist (Figure 10.24) as they share a similar morphology. The tibial plateau of a butchered pig knee or an unfused proximal tibial epiphysis may be easily identified when a portion of the proximal pig fibula is also available for examination. However, if only the very top of the tibial plateau is available without the shaft of the tibia, it can be very difficult to differentiate from a human tibia. Conversely,

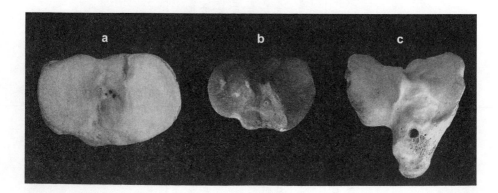

Figure 10.24   Comparison of a (a) human tibial plateau with that of (b) a pig, and (c) deer.

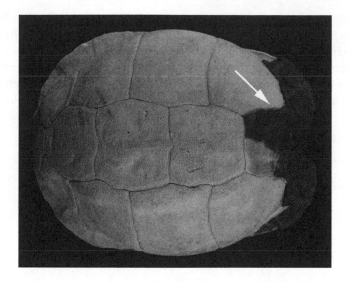

Figure 10.25 Turtle shell with an arrow indicating the remaining outer cover, referred to as a scute.

the tibial plateau of the deer is easily differentiated from the human knee because of the strikingly different morphology (Figure 10.24).

When the outer layer of a turtle shell, made up of pieces called scutes, comes off, the underlying shell may resemble the top of a human skull. This is particularly true if only part of the top of the shell is visible through the soil and has been bleached from sun exposure (Figure 10.25). Also, fragments of

Figure 10.26 Comparison between (a) a turtle shell fragment and (b) a human cranial fragment; both from archaeological contexts.

turtle shell from archaeological contexts can be easily mistaken for fragments of human cranial bone (Figure 10.26) because the flat shape and thickness is similar to human cranial vault fragments. If there are no diagnostic characteristics on the outside of the turtle shell fragment, then the cross-sectional morphology of the shell can be used to differentiate it from the unique cross section of human cranial bones, which are composed of diploe, or cancellous bone.

Appendix 1

Basic Equipment Checklist

- ❑ Survey transit, tripod, and stadia rod
- ❑ Hand compass
- ❑ 30–50 meter field tapes (at least 2)
- ❑ 5-meter steel pocket tape
- ❑ Folding stick ruler
- ❑ Plumb bob and line levels
- ❑ Large nails, wooden stakes, and chaining stakes
- ❑ Survey string, flagging tape, and survey flags
- ❑ Metal/rubber mallet and hand tools (multipurpose tool)
- ❑ Pocketknife
- ❑ Machete or handsaw
- ❑ Loppers
- ❑ Soil probe and corer
- ❑ Flat and spade shovels, and a leaf rake
- ❑ Wisk broom and dustpans
- ❑ Plastic buckets
- ❑ Trowels
- ❑ Root clippers
- ❑ Bamboo skewers and tablespoons
- ❑ Natural bristle brushes
- ❑ Large screen (at least 24" × 30" exposed mesh)
- ❑ Small screen (fine mesh for screening tiny items)
- ❑ Tweezers and magnifying glass
- ❑ Plastic tarps and rope
- ❑ Photographic gear, north arrow, and photo scale
- ❑ Field notebook, drawing supplies, and photo scale
- ❑ Blank forms
- ❑ Paper bags and tags

Appendix 2

Entomology Kit Checklist

- ❑ Large tackle box
- ❑ 6 pairs of disposable gloves
- ❑ 12" collapsible net with handle extension
- ❑ 2" magnifying lens
- ❑ Photo scale
- ❑ Plastic garden trowel
- ❑ Standard 4.5" trowel
- ❑ Paper towels
- ❑ Cotton balls
- ❑ 6" in/out thermometer with case
- ❑ 4-oz. bottle ethyl alcohol solution
- ❑ 4-oz. bottle purified water
- ❑ 2-oz. bottle KAAD larval fixative
- ❑ 1/8 in mesh small frame screen
- ❑ 1/4 in mesh small frame screen
- ❑ Vial forceps
- ❑ Featherweight forceps
- ❑ Metal probe
- ❑ 2 camel hair brushes
- ❑ 6 – 4-oz. kill jars
- ❑ 4 – 9-oz. kill jars
- ❑ 25 – 4-dram vials
- ❑ 20 bait cups with lids
- ❑ Entomology labels
- ❑ 20 white scale cards
- ❑ 10 disposable wood spatulas
- ❑ Small pack of vermiculite
- ❑ Pack of foil potato wrappers
- ❑ Small funnel
- ❑ No. 2 pencils
- ❑ Grease pencil
- ❑ Hand sanitizer
- ❑ Insect ID cards

Appendix 3

Entomology Notation and Collection Checklist

Above Ground Recoveries
- ❑ Notation of scene characteristics
- ❑ Notation of insect infestation
- ❑ Temperature data collection
- ❑ Collection of preserved adult flies and beetles near body
- ❑ Collection of preserved adult flies and beetles away from the body
- ❑ Collection of preserved eggs, larvae, and puparia
- ❑ Collection of live eggs and larvae
- ❑ Collection of specimens directly under the body and in close proximity to the body

Buried Remains
- ❑ Notation of scene characteristics
- ❑ Notation of insect infestation
- ❑ Temperature data collection
- ❑ Collection of preserved adult flies and beetles near burial
- ❑ Collection of preserved adult flies and beetles away from the burial
- ❑ Sift back fill for entomological evidence
- ❑ Collection of preserved eggs, larvae, and puparia
- ❑ Collection of live eggs and larvae
- ❑ Sift soil directly under body and the sides of the burial for entomological material

Appendix 4

Entomology Specimen Log Sheet

Case # _____
Agency _____
Date _____

Specimen #	Description	Collected By

Appendix 5

Entomology Data Form
(After Byrd, 2001)

Date: _____ Case #:_____

County/State: _____Agency: _____

Decedent: _____Age: _____ Sex: _____

Last seen alive: _____Time and date found: _____

Date reported missing: _____Time removed from scene: _____

Site description:

_____

_____

Crime Scene Area:

Rural:
- ❏ forest
- ❏ barren area
- ❏ open building

- ❏ pasture
- ❏ closed building
- ❏ other

- ❏ brush
- ❏ roadside

Urban/Suburban:
- ❏ closed building
- ❏ pavement

- ❏ open building
- ❏ trash container

- ❏ vacant lot
- ❏ other

Aquatic habitat:
- ❏ pond
- ❏ small river
- ❏ ditch
- ❏ drainage ditch
- ❏ brackish water

- ❏ lake
- ❏ large river
- ❏ gulf
- ❏ salt water
- ❏ other _____

- ❏ creek
- ❏ irrigation canal
- ❏ swampy area
- ❏ fresh water

Exposure:

❑ open air   ❑ burial (depth: _____)
❑ entire clothing   ❑ partial clothing   ❑ nude
Portion of body clothed:_____
Description of clothing:_____
Type of debris on body:_____

Decomposition stage:
❑ fresh   ❑ bloat   ❑ active decay
❑ advanced decay   ❑ skeletonized   ❑ adipocere
❑ mummification   ❑ dismemberment   ❑ other

Evidence of scavengers:_____

Possible traumatic
  injury sites:

_____

_____

_____

Scene Temperatures:
ambient_____   ambient (1 ft)_____   body surface_____
ground surface_____   under body_____   maggot mass_____
water temp_____   enclosed area_____   AC/Heat: on/
                                                          off_____
soil temp 10cm_____   soil temp 20cm_____   ceiling fan on/
                                                          off_____

Number of preserved samples_____
Number of live samples_____

Appendix 6

Entomological Preservation Solutions (Terrestrial)

Ethyl Alcohol (Ethanol)

This alcohol is best suited for killing and preserving adult specimens and for preserving larval specimens after fixing. It is also suitable for preservation of most eggs, larvae, and pupae of aquatic insects. It is purchased in bulk at 95% concentrations and should be diluted for entomological purposes to a solution of 75 to 80%. Adding 15 parts distilled water to 80 parts 95% ethanol will produce an 80% solution.

K.A.A. (KAAD)

95% ethanol	80 to 100 ml
Glacial acetic acid	20 ml
Kerosene	10 ml

This solution is only used for killing larval specimens, and can also be used for aquatic specimens. Specimens will become brittle if they are left in this solution for longer than 12 hours. After specimens are killed, they should be transferred into a 75 to 80% solution of ethanol.

Kahle's Solution

95% ethanol	30 ml
Formaldehyde	12 ml
Glacial Acetic Acid	4 ml
Water	60 ml

This solution can be used for killing and preserving adult specimens and for preserving larval specimens.

Source: Adapted from Byrd (2001)

Appendix 7

Measurement Equivalents and Conversion Factors

Length	Equivalent
1 meter	= 1.09361 yards
1 meter	= 39.37 inches
1 meter	= 3.28 feet
1 centimeter	= 0.394 inches
1 kilometer	= 0.6214 miles
1 kilometer	= 1,093.61 yards
1 yard	= 0.9144 meters
1 foot	= 0.3048 meters
1 inch	= 2.54 centimeters
1 mile	= 1,609.35 meters

Area	Equivalent
1 square meter	= 1.19598 square yards
1 square yard	= 0.836 square meters
1 square foot	= 0.0929 square meters
1 square inch	= 645.16 square millimeters
1 acre	= 4,046.9 square meters
1 hectare	= 2.47104 acres
1 square mile	= 2.59 square kilometers

Weight	Equivalent
1 kilogram	= 2.2 pounds
1 gram	= 0.035 ounces
1 ounce	= 28.3 grams
1 pound	= 0.455 kilograms
1 metric ton	= 1,000 kilograms

Volume	Equivalent
1 liter	= 1.0567 quarts
1 liter	= 0.2643 gallons
1 quart	= 0.9464 liters
1 gallon	= 3.785 liters
1 pint	= 0.95 liters

Standard	Equivalent
Length	
1 foot (ft)	= 12 inches (in)
1 yard (yd)	= 3 feet
1 mile (mi)	= 1,760 yards

Metric	Equivalent
Length	
1 centimeter (cm)	= 10 millimeters (mm)
1 meter (m)	= 100 centimeters (cm)
1 kilometer (km)	= 1,000 meters

(Continued)

Standard	Equivalent
Area	
1 square foot (ft²)	= 144 square inches
1 square yard (yd²)	= 9 square feet
1 acre	= 4,840 square yards
1 square mile (mi²)	= 640 acres
Volume	
1 cubic foot (ft³)	= 1,728 cubic in
1 cubic yard (yd³)	= 27 cubic feet
Capacity (Liquid and Dry Volumes)	
1 quart	= 2 pints
1 gallon	= 4 quarts
1 gallon	= 4 quarts

Metric	Equivalent
Area	
1 square cm (cm²)	= 100 square mm (mm²)
1 square m	= 1,000 square m (m²)
1 hectare	= 10,000 square m
1 square kilometer (km²)	= 1,000,000 square m
Volume	
1 cubic cm (cc or cm³)	= 1 milliliter (ml)
1 liter (l)	= 1,000 milliliters
1 cubic meter (m³)	= 1,000 liters
Capacity (Liquid and Dry Volumes)	
1 centiliter (cl)	= 10 milliliters
1 liter (l)	= 100 centiliters
1 kiloliter (kl)	= 1,000 liters

Convert	Into	Multiply by
Length		
Inches	centimeters	2.54
Feet	meters	0.3048
Miles	kilometers	1.609
Yards	meters	0.9144
Area		
Square inches	square centimeters	6.452
Square feet	square meters	0.0929

Convert	Into	Multiply by
Length		
Centimeters	inches	0.3937
Meters	feet	3.2808
Kilometers	miles	0.6214
Meters	yards	1.0936
Area		
Square centimeters	sq. inches	0.155
Square meters	sq. feet	10.76

(Continued)

Convert	Into	Multiply by
Acres	hectares	0.04047
Square miles	square kilometers	2.590
Square yards	square meters	0.8361
Volume		
Cubic inches	cubic cm	16.39
Cubic feet	cubic meters	0.02832
Cubic yards	cubic meters	0.7646
Capacity (Liquid and Dry Volumes)		
Pints	liters	0.5683
Gallons	liters	4.546

Convert	Into	Multiply by
Hectares	acres	2.471
square kilometers	square miles	0.3861
square meters	square yards	1.196
Volume		
Cubic cm	cubic inches	0.061
Cubic meters	cubic feet	35.31
Cubic meters	cubic yards	1.196
Capacity (Liquid and Dry Volumes)		
Liters	pints	1.76
Liters	gallons	0.22

MAP SCALE EQUIVALENTS

Map scale	Inches to mile	Feet to an inch	Km to an inch
1:6,000	105.6	50	0.0153
1:1,200	52.8	100	0.0305
1:2,400	26.4	200	0.061
1:2,500	25.34	208.3	0.0635
1:3,600	17.6	300	0.0914
1:4,800	13.2	400	0.1219
1:6,000	10.56	500	0.1524
1:10,000	6.34	833.3	0.254
1:20,000	3.17	1,666	0.508
1:25,000	2.53	2,083	0.635
1:100,000	0.634	8,333	2.54
1:500,000	0.1267	41,666	12.7
1:1,000,000	0.063	83,333.3	25.4

Appendix 8

Hypotenuse Table for Constructing Grids

	1	1.5	2	2.5	3	3.5	4	4.5	5	5.5	6	6.5	7	7.5	8	8.5	9	9.5	10
1	1.414	1.803	2.236	2.693	3.162	3.640	4.123	4.610	5.099	5.590	6.083	6.576	7.071	7.566	8.062	8.559	9.055	9.552	10.05
1.5	1.803	2.121	2.500	2.915	3.354	3.808	4.272	4.743	5.220	5.701	6.185	6.671	7.159	7.649	8.139	8.631	9.124	9.618	10.11
2	2.236	2.500	2.828	3.202	3.606	4.031	4.472	4.924	5.385	5.852	6.324	6.801	7.280	7.762	8.246	8.732	9.220	9.708	10.20
2.5	2.693	2.915	3.202	3.356	3.905	4.301	4.717	5.148	5.590	6.042	6.500	6.964	7.433	7.906	8.382	8.860	9.341	9.823	10.31
3	3.162	3.354	3.606	3.905	4.243	4.610	5.000	5.408	5.831	6.265	6.708	7.159	7.616	8.078	8.544	9.014	9.487	9.962	10.44
3.5	3.640	3.808	4.031	4.301	4.610	4.950	5.315	5.701	6.103	6.519	6.946	7.382	7.826	8.276	8.732	9.192	9.657	10.12	10.59
4	4.123	4.272	4.472	4.717	5.000	5.315	5.657	6.021	6.403	6.800	7.211	7.632	8.062	8.500	8.944	9.394	9.849	10.31	10.77
4.5	4.610	4.743	4.924	5.148	5.408	5.701	6.021	6.364	6.727	7.106	7.500	7.906	8.322	8.746	9.179	9.618	10.06	10.51	10.97
5	5.099	5.220	5.385	5.590	5.831	6.103	6.403	6.727	7.071	7.433	7.810	8.201	8.602	9.014	9.434	9.862	10.30	10.74	11.18
5.5	5.590	5.701	5.852	6.042	6.265	6.519	6.800	7.106	7.433	7.778	8.139	8.515	8.902	9.301	9.708	10.12	10.55	10.98	11.41
6	6.083	6.185	6.324	6.500	6.708	6.946	7.211	7.500	7.810	8.139	8.485	8.846	9.220	9.605	10.00	10.40	10.82	11.24	11.66

(Continued)

(Continued)

	1	1.5	2	2.5	3	3.5	4	4.5	5	5.5	6	6.5	7	7.5	8	8.5	9	9.5	10
6.5	6.576	6.671	6.801	6.964	7.159	7.382	7.632	7.906	8.201	8.515	8.846	9.192	9.552	9.925	10.31	10.70	11.10	11.51	11.93
7	7.081	7.159	7.280	7.433	7.616	7.826	8.062	8.322	8.602	8.902	9.220	9.552	9.899	10.26	10.63	11.01	11.40	11.80	12.21
7.5	7.566	7.649	7.762	7.906	8.078	8.276	8.500	8.746	9.014	9.301	9.605	9.925	10.26	10.61	10.97	11.34	11.72	12.10	12.50
8	8.062	8.139	8.246	8.382	8.544	8.732	8.944	9.179	9.434	9.708	10.00	10.31	10.63	10.97	11.31	11.67	12.04	12.42	12.81
8.5	8.559	8.631	8.732	8.860	9.014	9.192	9.394	9.618	9.862	10.12	10.40	10.70	11.01	11.34	11.67	12.02	12.38	12.75	13.12
9	9.055	9.124	9.220	9.341	9.487	9.657	9.849	10.06	10.30	10.55	10.82	11.10	11.40	11.72	12.04	12.38	12.73	13.09	13.45
9.5	9.552	9.618	9.708	9.823	9.962	10.12	10.31	10.51	10.74	10.98	11.24	11.51	11.80	12.10	12.42	12.75	13.09	13.44	13.79
10	10.05	10.11	10.20	10.31	10.44	10.59	10.77	10.97	11.18	11.41	11.66	11.93	12.21	12.50	12.81	13.12	13.45	13.79	14.14

Appendix 9

Adult Skeletal Inventory Form

Recording Key

Present:
Fracture: Fx
Carnivore Activity: C
Case Number: _____Date: _____
Recorder: _____

Single Bones:

Cranium	_____	Cervical Vertebra 3-7	_____
Mandible	_____	Thoracic Vertebra 1-12	_____
Hyoid	_____	Sacrum	_____
Manubrium	_____	Coccyx Vertebra 1-4	_____
Sternum	_____		
C1 (Atlas)	_____		
C2 (Axis)	_____		

Paired Bones:

	Right	Left		Right	Left
Clavicle	_____	_____	Ribs	_____	_____
Scapula	_____	_____	Innominate	_____	_____
Humerus	_____	_____	Femur	_____	_____
Radius	_____	_____	Patella	_____	_____
Ulna	_____	_____	Tibia	_____	_____
Lunate	_____	_____	Fibula	_____	_____
Scaphoid	_____	_____	Calcaneus	_____	_____
Trapezium	_____	_____	Talus	_____	_____
Trapezoid	_____	_____	Cuboid	_____	_____
Triquetral	_____	_____	Navicular	_____	_____
Hamate	_____	_____	Cuneiform 1	_____	_____
Capitate	_____	_____	Cuneiform 2	_____	_____
Pisiform	_____	_____	Cuneiform 3	_____	_____
Metacarpals	_____	_____	Metatarsals	_____	_____
Phalanges	_____	_____	Phalanges	_____	_____

Appendix 10

Adult Skeleton Inventory Image

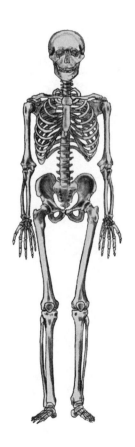

Appendix 11

Juvenile Skeleton Inventory Image

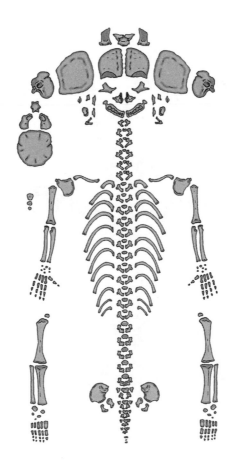

Glossary

Alveolus A relatively large projection or prominent bump.

Apical Toward the tip of the root of the tooth.

Appendicular skeleton All the bones of the limbs.

Archaeology The study of past societies through material remains (e.g., pottery, stone tools, art, and architecture).

Articulation The region where adjacent bones contact each other, usually forming a joint surface. To be truly articulated bones must have soft tissue connecting them. Although some individuals may use the term *articulated* to describe an undisturbed skeleton, it is more correct to describe the skeleton as being in *anatomical position*.

Auditory ossicles Paired bones of the ears that consist of the incus (anvil), stapes (stirrup), and malleus (hammer). These bones are found within the temporal bones.

Axial skeleton Bones of the thorax (including the shoulder girdle, ribs, vertebrae, and pelvis).

Benchmark A precisely determined point of elevation established in the field by licensed surveyors and made of stamped brass disks that are affixed to rock outcroppings, bridges, buildings, or other prominent and permanent features.

Bioturbation Mixing, displacement, or modification of the position of materials in the soil.

Buccal Surface of the molars and premolars that face the cheek.

Burial site A location where intentional human interments (burials) are found.

Cancellous bone The spongy or honeycomb structure of bone tissue typically found at the ends of long bones. Also referred to as trabecular or spongy bone.

Carpals Bones of the wrist. Each wrist has eight carpals arranged in two rows. The proximal row (from lateral to medial) consists of the scaphoid, lunate, triquetral, and pisiform. The distal row (from lateral to medial) consists of the trapezium, trapezoid, capitate, and hamate.

Cemento-enamel junction (CEJ)   The point at which the enamel of the tooth crown ends and the cementum of the tooth root begins.

Cementum   The soft tissue covering tooth roots that anchors them to the periodontal ligament.

Cervical vertebrae   There are seven cervical vertebrae that comprise the most superior portion of the vertebral column. The first cervical vertebra is often referred to as the atlas, while the second is commonly referred to as the axis. The cervical vertebrae may be abbreviated as C1, C2, etc., with C1 as the most superior.

Circular or spiral search pattern   A search pattern in which the searcher moves in decreasing concentric circles (outside toward the inside).

Clavicle   Paired bones (also known as the collar bone), found in the upper-thorax region.

Coccyx   Comprised of four or five fused or unfused elements. The coccyx is also known as the tailbone, and it is found inferior to the sacrum.

Condyle   A large, rounded, articular process.

Context   The physical setting, location, and cultural association of an object (skeletal material or associated evidence) and features within an archaeological site or crime scene.

Control-point mapping   A map that records the position of objects in relation to a known point.

Cortical bone   The dense, thickened, outer layer of bone. Also referred to as compact bone.

Cranial skeleton   All the components of the skull (sometimes including the hyoid).

Cremation   A process that uses intense heat to rapidly reduce a body to ashes and small bone fragments.

Crest   A prominent ridge of bone that is commonly associated with muscle or ligament attachment.

Crown   Upper portion of the tooth that is visible in the mouth.

Cultural anthropology   The study of human society (usually living societies), including but not limited to social structure, behavior, beliefs, and ways of life.

Cusp   A small elevation on the occlusal surface of a tooth (primarily found on the premolars and molars).

Datum   A fixed point of reference for all depth and angle measurements made during the recovery of human remains and other associated evidence.

Dentin   Internal tissue in a tooth crown and root, surrounding the pulp cavity and surrounded by the crown enamel. This bone-like substance is softer than the enamel.

Diaphysis   The shaft of the long bone.

Distal   In bones, distal is the end of the long bone farthest from the axial skeleton. Used to describe bones of the appendicular skeleton. In the dentition, distal is opposite of mesial, or toward the back of the mouth.

Electromagnetic meter (EM)   Also referred to as a conductivity meter, the EM transmitter projects a primary electromagnetic field into the ground that will generate small eddy currents on the surface of conducting objects (ferrous and nonferrous) or features, and the eddy currents in turn create a secondary magnetic field that is measured by the receiver.

Enamel   The hard, white mineral portion of the tooth that makes up the majority of the tooth crown.

Epiphyseal growth plate   The soft tissue structure (cartilage) located between the metaphysis and the epiphysis.

Epiphysis   Found at the ends of the long bones. During growth, the epiphyses are initially separated from the metaphysis by a layer of cartilage that eventually ossifies and fuses the parts together.

Ethmoid   Single bone found in the superior portion of the nasal cavity. This bone is very fragile and, from the exterior of the cranium, it is only visible on the medial aspect of the eye orbits.

Facet   A small, smooth, articular surface.

Feature   A large stationary artifact, such as a firepit, human burial, housepit, cairn, bedrock mortar, or an association of related portable artifacts such as a cache.

Femur   Paired bones that make up the proximal part of the leg (also known as the thigh bone).

Fibula   Paired bones that are found on the lateral side of the lower leg.

Foramen   An opening or hole that goes through a bone.

Forensic anthropology   The application of theory and methods from physical anthropology to answer questions posed in a legal sphere.

Forensic archaeology   Use of standard archaeological principles and methods to locate and recover human remains and associated evidence within the context of a forensic investigation.

Forensic botany   The application of information taken from plants to answer questions in legal investigations.

Forensic entomology   The use of insect evidence to answer questions pertaining to legal issues.

Forensic palynology   A subdiscipline of forensic botany that uses pollen spores to help solve crimes.

Fossa   A broad, shallow, depressed area.

Frontal   Single bone found in the forehead region of the cranium.

Frontal (coronal) plane   Plane of reference that separates the body into a front and back half.

Geophysical survey   The study of locating and mapping objects or features that are underground or underwater.

Geotaphonomy   The use of archaeological techniques to recognize specific geophysical characteristics and changes that affect the burial feature and the surrounding environment.

Global Information Systems (GIS)   Computer software used for mapping and analyzing spatial or geographical data.

Global Positioning System (GPS)   A satellite-based navigation system placed into orbit by the U.S. Department of Defense.

Grid mapping   A map in which grid squares are used to mark the limits of a site, control the work area, and record evidence in great detail.

Grid search pattern   A variation of the strip or line search. Once the team has completed the line search pattern, the team will search the same area in a perpendicular direction.

Groove (sulcus)   A deep or shallow trench on a bone that during life may contain a tendon or vessel.

Ground penetrating radar (GPR)   An active geophysical survey tool that emits electromagnetic pulses to locate disturbances underground.

Humerus   Paired bones that make up the upper arm.

Hyoid   Single, U-shaped bone that is found inferior to the mandible.

Incisal   Chewing surface of the incisors.

Inferior   Away from the cranium (may also be referred to as caudal). Used to describe bones of the axial skeleton.

Infracranial skeleton   All the bones of the skeleton below the skull.

In situ   When skeletal remains and associated evidence are found in the location where they were last deposited.

Labial   Surface of the incisors and canines that faces the lips.

Lacrimal   Paired bones located on the inferior and medial aspect of the eye orbits. These small fragile bones house the tear glands during life.

Lateral   Away from the midline of the body.

Line (ridge)   A long, thin projection of bone, often with a rough surface and usually associated with muscle attachment.

Lingual   Surface of the tooth that faces the tongue.

Linguistics   The study of how languages evolve and the relationships between languages and the societies that use them.

Lumbar vertebrae   There are five lumbar vertebrae that are located inferior to the thoracic vertebrae and superior to the sacrum. The lumbar vertebrae are often abbreviated as L1 through L5, with L1 as the most superior.

Maggot   The larva of the housefly and blowfly that can commonly be found in decaying organic matter.

Magnetic detector   Designed to locate the magnetic field of ferromagnetic objects.

Magnetometer (MAG)   Used to detect the magnetic field of ferromagnetic objects.

Mandible   Single bone, also referred to as the lower jaw.

Manubrium   The most superior portion of the sternum, sometimes found as a separate bone.

Maxilla   Paired bones that make up the upper jaw.

Medial   Toward the midline of the body.

Medullary cavity   The inner cavity of the long bone, which in life provides storage for yellow marrow (fat) and is also the center for the production of red blood cells.

Mesial   In the dentition, mesial is toward the midline of the mouth.

Metacarpal   Bones of the palm of the hand. Each hand has five metacarpals that are numbered 1 through 5 starting with the lateral (base of the thumb). Metacarpals are commonly abbreviated as MT1, MT2, etc.

Metal detector   Electromagnetic devices that operate on the same principle as electromagnetic surveying equipment.

Metaphysis   The growing and expanded portion of a long bone shaft between the diaphysis and the epiphyseal ends of the long bone where the growth plate is located and where the epiphyses will eventually fuse.

Metatarsals   There are five metatarsals in each foot. These bones make up the arch of the foot. The metatarsals are sometimes abbreviated as MT1, MT2, etc., starting with the medial side under the big toe.

Multiple burials   A burial that consists of a single grave that contains the remains of two or more individuals.

Nasal   Paired bones that make up the bridge of the nose.

Nasal concha   Paired bones located on the lateral aspects of the nasal cavity.

Nutrient foramen   A small hole or channel that penetrates the bone. It facilitates the entrance of blood vessels and nerves into the bone.

Oblique plane   Plane of reference that is found at any other angle on the body.

Occipital   Single bone that makes up the back and bottom of the cranium. The large foramen magnum is located on this bone.

Occlusal   Chewing surfaces of all the teeth.

Orientation   The direction in which the head lies in relation to the body's central axis; should be recorded in directional terms using a compass or in reference to natural or human-made features.

Palatine   Paired bones that make up the posterior aspect of the roof of the mouth and the posterior aspect of the floor of the nasal cavity.

Parietal   Paired bones found on the right and left side of the superior portion of the cranium.

Patella   Paired bones found in the knee (also called the knee bone).

Pelvis   The pelvis is comprised of two pelvic bones (also called *os coxae* or innominates). These bones are also called the hipbones.

Perimortem   At or around the time of death.

Periodontal ligament   Soft tissue ligament that holds the tooth into the tooth socket.

Periosteum   The soft tissue fibrous membrane that covers the bone.

Phalange   Bones of the fingers and toes. Each hand and each foot has a total of 14 phalanges that are divided into three groups based on their location. There are five proximal phalanges per hand and foot, four intermediate phalanges (the thumb and the big toe lack intermediate phalanges), and five distal or terminal phalanges.

Physical/biological anthropology   The study of the physical and biological aspects of the primate order; includes past and present studies of humans and nonhuman primates.

Position   The relationship of the legs, arms, and head to each other and to the trunk of the body in a burial context.

Postmortem   After death.

Postmortem interval (PMI)   The amount of time that has passed since death.

Premortem (or antemortem)   Before death.

Primary burial   A burial in which the body and skeletal remains remain in their original position and the context of the burial has not been disturbed.

Process   A projection of bone.

Prone   Body position in which the palms of the hands are facing backward, causing the radius to be crossed over the ulna.

Provenience   The horizontal and/or vertical position of an object in relation to a set of spatial coordinates.

Proximal   End of the long bone closest to the axial portion of the body. Used to describe bones of the appendicular skeleton.

Pulp chamber   The inner portion of the tooth that contains the blood and nerve supply.

Puparia   The life stage of an insect between the larva (maggot) and the adult.

Radius   Paired bones that are found in the lower arm on the lateral side when the body is in standard anatomical position.

Ribs   There are 12 pairs of ribs that make up the rib cage. The ribs articulate posteriorly with the thoracic vertebrae, and anteriorly with the sternum (except for ribs 11 and 12).

Root   The portion of a tooth that is embedded in the jaw and serves as support.

Sacrum   Comprised of five fused elements, the sacrum is located at the base of the vertebral column and between the two pelvic bones.

Sagittal (medial) plane   Plane of reference that is found down the middle of the body, cutting the body into a right and left half.

Scapula   Paired bones (also known as the shoulder blade) located on the superior portion of the back. These bones provide an anchor for the arm.

Secondary burial   A burial in which the skeletal remains have been removed from their original burial location by human activity and deposited in another location.

Sectional drawing   A drawing used to depict depth relations between objects.

Side-scan sonar   A marine geophysical tool that uses sound waves to produce a detailed graphic image, similar to an aerial image, of the surface of the seafloor, riverbed, or lake-bottom.

Sinus   A cavity or hollow area within a cranial bone.

Soil horizon   A layer of soil or soil material approximately parallel to the land surface and differing from adjacent layers in physical, chemical, and biological properties or characteristics (e.g., color, structure, and texture).

Sphenoid   Singular bone of the cranium. This is the most complex bone of the cranium, and it can be seen on the posterior aspect of the eye orbits, exteriorly on the sides of the cranium behind the eye orbits, and adjoining the palatine bones.

Spine   A relatively long, thin projection or bump.

Stadia rod   A long, painted rod that is accurately calibrated in metric units or standard units that is used for obtaining elevations and stadia measurements of distance in mapping with a major surveying instrument such as a transit.

Standard anatomical position Body faces forward, with palms facing forward so that all bones are visible (no bones are crossed over one another). Also referred to as the supine position.

Sternum Comprised of three fused or unfused elements called the manubrium, sternal body, and the xiphoid process. The sternum is located in the midline of the chest and is the anterior anchor site for the ribs.

Stratigraphy The arrangement of strata (layers of the earth), especially as to geographic position and chronologic order of sequence.

Strip or line search pattern Searchers line up in a straight line and are positioned close enough so that their field of vision overlaps. Individuals will search an area by walking first in one direction, and then in the opposite direction.

Subchondral bone Bone located at the joint that is covered by cartilage during life.

Superior Toward the cranium (may also be referred to as cephalic). Used to describe bones of the axial skeleton.

Supine Body position in which the palms of the hand are facing forward, causing the radius and ulna to be parallel to one another.

Surface deposit When human remains are left to decompose on the surface of the ground.

Suture Articulation or joints between the cranial bones.

Taphonomy The postmortem time period and modifications that occur to bodies and skeletal remains after death.

Tarsals Bones of the ankle. There are seven tarsal bones in each foot. The proximal row consists of the calcaneus, talus and navicular. The distal row (from medial to lateral) consists of the 1st cuneiform, 2nd cuneiform, 3rd cuneiform, and the cuboid.

Temporal Paired bones located on each side of the cranium. The temporals hold the auditory ossicles.

Thoracic vertebrae There are 12 thoracic vertebrae that are located inferior to the cervical vertebrae and superior to the lumbar vertebrae. These vertebrae hold the 12 pairs of ribs. The thoracic vertebrae are commonly abbreviated as T1 through T12, with T1 being the most superior.

Tibia Paired bones that make up the medial portion of the lower leg.

Total station An optical instrument used in modern surveying and mapping. It is a combination electronic transit (theodolite) and electronic distance-meauring device (EDM). With this device one may determine angles and distances from the instrument to points to be surveyed.

Transit (also known as a theodolite) A surveying and mapping instrument used for measuring horizontal and vertical angles.

Transverse (horizontal) plane Plane of reference that separates the body into upper and lower parts (can be found at any location along the body and is perpendicular to the sagittal and coronal planes).

Trochanter One of two specific tuberosities located on the femur.

Tubercle A projection or bump with a roughened surface (usually associated with muscle attachment), generally smaller than a tuberosity.

Tuberosity   A projection or bump with a roughened surface (associated with muscle attachment).

Ulna   Paired bones found on the medial side of the lower arm when in standard anatomical position.

Vomer   Single bone found in the midline of the nasal cavity.

Xiphoid process   The most inferior portion of the sternum. It is usually fused to the sternal body, but can also remain unfused.

Zygomatic   Paired bone, also known as malar or zygoma. This bone comprises the cheek area of the cranium.

References

Baker, B.J., T.L. Dupras, and M.W. Tocheri, *The Osteology of Infants and Children*, Texas A&M Press, College Station, TX, 2005.

Bass, W.M. The use of heavy power equipment in the excavation of human skeletal material, *Plains Anthropologist*, 8(20):122–123, 1963.

Bass, W.M., *Human Osteology: A Laboratory & Field Manual*, Missouri Archaeological Society, 1995.

Bass, W.M., *Death's Acre: Inside the Legendary Forensic Lab — The Body Farm — Where the Dead Do Tell Tales*, Putnam Publishing Group, New York, 2003.

Bass, W.M. and W.H. Birkby, Exhumation: the method can make the difference, *FBI Law Enforcement Bulletin*, 47:6–11, 1978.

Bates, D.M., G.J. Anderson, and R.D. Lee, Forensic botany: trichome evidence, *Journal of Forensic Science*, 42:380–386, 1997.

Behrensmeyer, A.K., Taphonomic and ecologic information from bone weathering, *Paleobiology*, 4:150–162, 1978.

Berryman, H.E., Disarticulation pattern and tooth mark artifacts associated with pig scavenging of human remains: a case study, in *Forensic Taphonomy: The Postmortem Fate of Human Remains*, W.D. Haglund and M.H. Sorg, Eds., CRC Press, Boca Raton, FL, 2002, pp. 487–495.

Berryman, H.E and C.H. Lahren, The advantages of simulated crime scenes in teaching forensic anthropology, *Journal of Forensic Science*, 20:699–700, 1984.

Bevan, B.W., The search for graves, *Geophysics*, 56:1310–1319, 1991.

Binford, L., *Bones: Ancient Men and Modern Myths*, Academic Press, New York, 1981.

Bock, J.H., M.A. Lane, and D.O. Norris, *The Use of Plant Cells in Forensic Investigation*, U.S. Department of Justice, National Institutes of Justice, 1988.

Bock, J.H. and D.O. Norris, A new application of plant anatomy, in *Strategies for Success in Anatomy and Physiology and Life Science*, No. 6, Benjamin/Cummings Publishing Co., San Francisco, 1991, pp. 6–8.

Bock, J.H. and D.O. Norris, Forensic botany: an underutilized resource, *American Journal of Botany*, 82: 105, 1995.

Bock, J.H. and D.O. Norris, Forensic botany: an under-utilized resource, *Journal of Forensic Science*, 42: 364–367, 1997.

Boyd, R.M., Buried body cases, *FBI Law Enforcement Bulletin*, 48(2):6–11, 1979.

Browning, M. and W.R. Maples, *Dead Men Do Tell Tales: The Strange and Fascinating Cases of a Forensic Anthropologist*, Main Street Books, New York, 1995.

Bryant, V.M., Jr., Pollen: Nature's Fingerprints of Plants, *1990 Yearbook of Science and the Future*, Encyclopedia Britannica, Chicago, 1989, pp. 92–111.

Bryant, V.M., Jr., D.C. Mildenhall, and J.G. Jones, Forensic palynology in the United States of America, *Palynology*, 4:193–208, 1990.

Burns, K.B., *Forensic Anthropology Training Manual*, Prentice-Hall, Upper Saddle River, NJ, 1998.

Byers, S.N., *Introduction to Forensic Anthropology: A Textbook*, 2nd ed., Allyn and Bacon, Boston, 2004.

Byrd, J.H., Laboratory rearing of forensic insects, in *Forensic Entomology: The Utility of Arthropods in Legal Investigations*, J.H. Byrd and J.L. Castner, Eds., CRC Press, Boca Raton, FL, 2001, pp. 121–142.

Byrd, J.H. and J.L. Castner, Insects of forensic importance, in *Forensic Entomology: The Utility of Arthropods in Legal Investigations*, J.H. Byrd and J.L. Castner, Eds., CRC Press, Boca Raton, FL, 2001a, pp. 43–79.

Byrd, J.H. and J.L. Castner, *Entomological Evidence: The Utility of Arthropods in Legal Investigations*, CRC Press, Boca Raton, 2001b.

Calkin, S.F., R.P. Allen, and M.P. Harriman, Buried in the basement; geophysic's role in forensic investigation, *Proceedings of the Symposium on the Application of Geophysics to Engineering and Environmental Problems (SAGEEP)*, pp. 397–403, 1995.

Carleton, M.D., Introduction to rodents, in *Orders and Families or Recent Mammals of the World*, S. Anderson, and K.J. Jones, Eds., John Wiley and Sons, Inc., New York, 1984, pp. 255–265.

Carson, E.A., V.H. Stefan, and J.F. Powell, Skeletal manifestations of bear scavenging, *Journal of Forensic Science*, 45(3):515–526, 2000.

Castner, J.L., General entomology and anthropod biology, in *Forensic Entomology: The Utility of Arthropods in Legal Investigations*, J.H. Byrd and J.L. Castner, Eds., CRC Press, Boca Raton, FL, 2001, pp. 17–41.

Conner, M. and D.D. Scott, Paradigms and perpetrators, *Historical Archaeology*, 35(1):1–6, 2001.

Conyers, L.B. and D. Goodman, *Ground-Penetrating Radar: An Introduction for Archaeologists*, AltaMira Press, Walnut Creek, CA, 1997.

Correia, P.M. and O. Beattie, A critical look at methods for recovering, evaluating, and interpreting cremated human remains, in *Advances in Forensic Taphonomy: Method, Theory, and Archaeological Perspectives*, W.D. Haglund and M.H. Sorg, Eds., CRC Press, Boca Raton, FL, 2002, pp. 435–450.

Davenport, C.G., Remote sensing applications in forensic investigations, *Historical Archaeology*, 35:87-100, 2001a.

Davenport, C.G., *Where Is It? Searching for Buried Bodies and Hidden Evidence*, Sport-Work, Church Hill, MD, 2001b.

Davis, J., Forensic archaeology, *Archaeology Review from Cambridge*, 11(1):151–156, 1992.

Davis, J.L. and A.P. Annan, Ground-penetrating radar for high-resolution mapping of soil and rock stratigraphy, *Geophysical Prospecting*, 37:531–551, 1989.

Davis, J.L., J.A. Hegginbottom, A.P. Annan, and K.E. Duncan, Plan view presentation of GPR data, *Seventh International Conference on Ground Penetrating Radar*, Lawrence, KS, 1998, pp 39–45.

Dirkmaat, D.C., Recovery and interpretation of the fatal fire victim: the role of forensic anthropology, in *Advances in Forensic Taphonomy: Method, Theory, and Archaeological Perspectives*, W.D. Haglund and M.H. Sorg, Eds., CRC Press, Boca Raton, FL, 2002, pp. 451–472.

Dirkmaat, D.C. and J.M. Adovasio, The role of archaeology in the recovery and interpretation of human remains from an outdoor setting, in *Forensic Taphonomy: The Postmortem Fate of Human Remains*, W.D. Haglund and M.H. Sorg, Eds., CRC Press, Boca Raton, FL, 1997, pp. 39–64.

Duncan, J., Search techniques, in *Handbook of Forensic Archaeology and Anthropology.* D. Morse, J. Duncan, and J. Stoutamire, Eds., Rose Printing, Tallahassee, FL, 1983, pp. 4–19.

Faegri, K., J. Iverson, and K. Krzywinski, *Textbook of Pollen Analysis, 4th ed.*, John Wiley & Sons, New York, 1989.

Fairgrieve, S.I. and J.E. Molto, Burning point: Canadian case studies of intentionally cremated human remains, in *Strength in Diversity: A Reader in Physical Anthropology*, A. Herring and L. Chan, Eds., Canadian Scholars' Press, Toronto, 1994, pp. 385–402.

France, D.L., T.J. Griffin, J.G. Swanburg, J.W. Lindemann, G.C. Davenport, V. Trammell, C.T. Travis, R. Kondratieff, A. Nelson, K. Castellano, and D. Hopkins, A multidisciplinary approach to the detection of clandestine graves, *Journal of Forensic Science*, 37:1445–1458, 1992.

France D.L., T.J. Griffin, J.G. Swanburg, J.W. Lindemann, G.C. Davenport, V. Trammell, C.T. Travis, R. Kondratieff, A. Nelson, K. Castellano, D. Hopkins, and T. Adair, NecroSearch revisited: further multidisciplinary approaches to the detection of clandestine graves, in *Forensic Taphonomy: The Postmortem Fate of Human Remains*, W.H. Haglund and M.H. Sorg, Eds., CRC Press, Boca Raton, FL, 1997, pp. 497–509.

Galloway, A., H. Walsh-Haney, and J. Byrd, Recovering buried bodies and surface scatter: the associated anthropological, botanical and entomological evidence, in *Forensic Entomology: The Utility of Arthropods in Legal Investigations*, J.H. Byrd and J.L. Castner, Eds., CRC Press, Boca Raton, FL, 2001, pp. 223–262.

Garett, C.L., *Modern Metal Detectors*, Ram Publishing Company, Dallas, 1998.

Gilbert, B.M., *Mammalian Osteology*, Missouri Archaeological Society, Columbia, MO, 1990.

Haglund, W.D., Rodents and human remains, in *Forensic Taphonomy: The Postmortem Fate of Human Remains*, W.D. Haglund and M.H. Sorg, Eds., CRC Press, Boca Raton, FL, 1997a, pp. 405–414.

Haglund, W.D., Scattered skeletal human remains: search strategy considerations for locating missing teeth, in *Forensic Taphonomy: The Postmortem Fate of Human Remains*, W.D. Haglund and M.H. Sorg, Eds., CRC Press, Boca Raton, FL, 1997b, pp. 383–394.

Haglund, W.D., Dogs and coyotes: postmortem involvement with human remains, in *Forensic Taphonomy: The Postmortem Fate of Human Remains*, W.D. Haglund and M.H. Sorg, Eds., CRC Press, Boca Raton, FL, 1997c, pp. 367–381.

Haglund, W.D., Recent mass graves, an introduction, in *Advances in Forensic Taphonomy: Method, Theory, and Archaeological Perspectives*, W.D. Haglund and M.H. Sorg, Eds., CRC Press, Boca Raton, FL, 2002, pp. 243–262.

Haglund, W.D. and M.H. Sorg, Method and theory of forensic taphonomic research, in *Forensic Taphonomy: The Postmortem Fate of Human Remains*, W.D. Haglund and M.H. Sorg, Eds., CRC Press, Boca Raton, FL, 1997, pp. 13–26.

Haglund, W.D, D.T. Reay, and D.R. Swindler, Tooth mark artifacts and survival of bones in animal scavenged human skeletons, *Journal of Forensic Science*, 33(4):985–997, 1988.

Hall, D.W., Contribution of the forensic botanist in crime scene investigations, *The Prosecutor,* 22(1): 35–38, 1988.

Hall, D.W., Forensic Botany, in *Forensic Taphonomy: The Postmortem Fate of Human Remains,* W.H. Haglund and M.H. Sorg, Eds., CRC Press, Boca Raton, FL, 1997, pp. 353–366.

Hall, R.D., Medicocriminal entomology, in *Entomology and Death: A Procedural Guide,* E.P. Catts and N.H. Haskell, Eds., Joyce's Print Shop, Clemson, SC, 1990, pp. 1–8.

Haskell, N.H. and E.P. Catts, *Entomology and Death: A Procedural Guide,* Joyce's Print Shop, Clemson, SC, 1990.

Haskell, N.H., W.D. Lord, and J.H. Byrd, Collection of entomological evidence during death investigations, in *Forensic Entomology: The Utility of Arthropods in Legal Investigations,* J.H. Byrd and J.L. Castner, Eds., CRC Press, Boca Raton, FL, 2001, pp. 81–120.

Haskell, N.H., R.D. Hall, V.J. Cervenka, and M.A. Clark, On the body: Insects' life stage presence and their postmortem artifacts, in *Forensic Taphonomy: The Postmortem Fate of Human Remains,* W.H. Haglund, and M.H. Sorg, Eds., CRC Press, Boca Raton, FL, 1997, pp. 415–448.

Haynes, G., Prey bones and predators: potential ecologic weathering from analysis of bone sites, *Ossa,* 7:75–97, 1980.

Hillson, S., *Teeth,* Cambridge University Press, New York, 1986.

Hillson, S., *Mammal Bones and Teeth: An Introductory Guide to Methods of Identification,* University of London Institute of Archaeology, London, 1992.

Hochrein, M.J., Buried crime scene evidence: the application of geotaphonomy in forensic archaeology, in *Forensic Dentistry,* P. Stimson and C. Mertz, Eds., CRC Press, Boca Raton, FL, 1997a, pp. 83–99.

Hochrein, M.J., The dirty dozen: the recognition and collection of toolmarks in the forensic geotaphonomic record, *Journal of Forensic Identification,* 47(2):171–198, 1997b.

Hochrein, M.J., Autopsy of the grave: recognizing, collecting, and preserving forensic geotaphonomic evidence, in *Advances in Forensic Taphonomy: Method, Theory, and Archaeological Perspectives,* W.D. Haglund, and M.H. Sorg, Eds., CRC Press, Boca Raton, FL, 2002, pp. 45–70.

Horrocks, M., S.A. Coulson, and K.A.J. Walsh, Forensic palynology: variation in the pollen content of soil surface samples, *Journal of Forensic Science,* 43(2):320–323, 1998.

Hoshower, L.M., Forensic archaeology and the need for flexible excavation strategies: a case study, *Journal of Forensic Science,* 43(1):53–56, 1998.

Hunter, J.R., A background to forensic archaeology, in *Studies in Crime: An Introduction to Forensic Archaeology,* J. Hunter, C. Roberts, and A. Martin, Eds., Routledge, London, 1996a, pp. 7–23.

Hunter, J.R., Locating buried remains, in *Studies in Crime: An Introduction to Forensic Archaeology,* J.R. Hunter, C.A. Roberts, and A.L. Martin, Eds., Routledge, London, 1996b, pp. 86–100.

Hunter, J.R., Foreword: A pilgrim in forensic archaeology — a personal view, in *Advances in Forensic Taphonomy: Method, Theory, and Archaeological Perspectives,* W.D. Haglund and M.H. Sorg, Eds., CRC Press, Boca Raton, FL, 2002, pp. xxv–xxxii.

Hunter, J., C. Roberts, and A. Martin, *Studies in Crime: An Introduction to Forensic Archaeology,* B.T. Batsford, London, 1996.

Hunter, J.R., C. Heron, R.C. Janaway, A.L. Martin, A.M. Pollard, and C.A. Roberts, Forensic archaeology in Britain, *Antiquity,* 68:758–769, 1994.

Imaizumi, M., Locating buried bodies, *FBI Law Enforcement Bulletin,* 43(8):2–5, 1974.

Iscan, M.Y., Global forensic anthropology in the 21st century, *Forensic Science International,* 117:1–6, 2001.

Iscan, M.Y. and B.Q. McCabe, Analysis of human remains recovered from a shark, *Forensic Science International*, 72(1):15–23, 1995.

Iserson, K.V., *Death to Dust: What Happens to Dead Bodies?* 2nd ed., Galen Press, Ltd., Tucson, AZ, 2001.

Jackson, D.M. and C. Fellenbaum, *The Bone Detectives: How Forensic Anthropologists Solve Crimes and Uncover Mysteries of the Dead*, Little, Brown & Co, Boston, 2001.

Killam, E.W., *The Detection of Human Remains*, Charles C. Thomas, Springfield, IL, 1990.

King, C.G. and S. King, The archaeology of fire investigation, *Fire Engineering* 142(6):70–74, 1989.

King, J.A., B.W. Bevan, and R.J. Hurry, The reliability of geophysical surveys at historic-period cemeteries: an example from the Plains Cemetery, Mechanicsville, Maryland, *Historical Archaeology* 27:4–16, 1993.

Ladd, C. and H. Lee, The use of biological and botanical evidence in criminal investigations, in *Forensic Botany: Principles and Applications to Criminal Casework*, H. Miller Coyle, Ed., CRC Press, Boca Raton, FL, 2004, pp. 97–116.

Lane, M.A., L.C. Anderson, T.M. Barkley, J.H. Bock, E.M. Gifford, D.W. Hall, D.O. Norris, T.L. Rost, and W.L. Stern, Forensic Botany: plants, perpetrators, pests, poisons and pot, *Bioscience*, 40:34–39, 1990.

Lord, W.D. and J.F. Burger, Collection and preservation of forensically important entomological materials, *Journal of Forensic Science*, 28:936–944, 1983.

Lowy, A. and P. McAlhany, Human remains detection: the latest police canine detector specialty, *FDIAI News*, April-June: 6–8, 2000.

Ludwig, J., *Handbook of Autopsy Practice*, Humana Press, Totowa, NJ, 2002.

Lyman, R.L., *Vertebrate Taphonomy*, Cambridge University Press, New York, 1994.

Maguire, J.M., D. Pemberton, and M.H. Collett, The Makapansgat Limeworks Grey Breccia: hominids, hyaenas, hystricids, or hillwash? *Paleontologia Africana*, 23:75–98, 1980.

Mellett, J.S., Location of human remains with ground-penetrating radar, *Geological Survey of Finland*, 16:359–365, 1992.

Micozzi, M.S., *Postmortem Change in Human and Animal Remains, A Systematic Approach*, Charles C. Thomas, Springfield, IL, 1991.

Mildenhall, D.C., Forensic palynology, *Geological Society of New Zealand Newsletter*, 58(25), 1982.

Mildenhall, D.C., Deer velvet and palynology: an example of the use of forensic palynology in New Zealand, *Tuatara*, 30:1–11, 1988.

Mildenhall, D.C., Forensic palynology in New Zealand, *Review of Palaeobotony and Palynology*, 64–65:227–234, 1990.

Mildenhall, D.C., Pollen plays part in crime-busting, *Forensic Focus*, 11:1–4, 1992.

Miller Coyle, H., Introduction to forensic botany, in *Forensic Botany: Principles and Applications to Criminal Casework*, H. Miller Coyle, Ed., CRC Press, Boca Raton, FL, 2004, pp. 1–8.

Milne, L.A., V.M. Bryant, and D.C. Mildenhall, Forensic palynology, in *Forensic Botany: Principles and Applications to Criminal Casework*, H. Miller Coyle, Ed., CRC Press, Boca Raton, FL, 2004, pp. 217–252.

Moore, W.J., *The Mammalian Skull*, Cambridge University Press, New York, 1981.

Morse, D., J. Duncan, and J. Stoutamire, *Handbook of Forensic Archaeology and Anthropology*, Rose Printing, Tallahassee, FL, 1983.

Murad, T.A., The growing popularity of cremation versus inhumation: some forensic implications, in *Forensic Osteology: Advances in the Identification of Human Remains*, 2nd ed., K. Reichs, Ed., Charles C. Thomas, Springfield, IL, 1998, pp. 86–105.

Nobes, D.C., The search for "Yvonne": a case example of the delineation of a grave using near-surface geophysical methods, *Journal of Forensic Science*, 45:715–21, 2000.

Norris, D.O. and J.H. Bock, Use of fecal material to associate a suspect with a crime scene: report of two cases, *Journal of Forensic Science*, 45:184–187, 2000.

Olsen, S.J., *Mammal Remains from Archaeological Sites. Part I: Southeastern and Southwestern United States*, Vol. 56, No. 1, Papers of the Peabody Museum of Archaeology and Ethnography, Harvard University Press, Cambridge, 1996.

Owsley, D.W., Techniques for locating burials, with emphasis on the probe, *Journal of Forensic Science*, 40:735–740, 1995.

Pain, S., Silent witnesses, *Kew*, Autumn:22–25, 1993.

Proctor, N.S. and P.J. Lynch, *Manual of Ornithology: Avian Structure and Function*, Yale University Press, New Haven, CT, 1993.

Rapp, G.R. and C.L. Hill, *Geoarchaeology: The Earth-Science Approach to Archaeological Interpretation*, Yale University Press, New Haven, CT, 1998.

Rathbun, T.A. and B.C. Rathbun, Human remains recovered from a shark's stomach in South Carolina, *Journal of Forensic Science*, 29:269–276, 1984.

Rebmann, A., E. David, and M.H. Sorg, *Cadaver Dog Handbook: Forensic Training and Tactics for the Recovery of Human Remains*, CRC Press, Boca Raton, FL, 2000.

Redsicker, D.R. and J.J. O'Connor, *Practical Fire and Arson Investigation*, 2nd ed., CRC Press, Boca Raton, FL, 1996.

Renfrew, C. and P. Bahn, *Archaeology: Theories, Methods and Practice*, Thames and Hudson, New York, 2000.

Reynolds, J.M., *An Introduction to Applied and Environmental Geophysics*, Willey and Sons, Inc., New York, 1997.

Rhine, S., *Bone Voyage: A Journey in Forensic Anthropology*, University of New Mexico Press, Albuquerque, New Mexico, 1998.

Roksandic, M., Position of skeletal remains as a key to understanding mortuary behavior, in *Advances in Forensic Taphonomy: Method, Theory, and Archaeological Perspectives*, W.D. Haglund and M.H. Sorg, Eds., CRC Press, Boca Raton, FL, 2002, pp. 99–118.

Rossi, M.L., A.W. Shahrom, R.C. Chapman, and P. Vanezis, Postmortem injury by indoor pets, *American Journal of Forensic Medicine and Pathology*, 15:105–109, 1994.

Scheuer, L. and S. Black, *Developmental Juvenile Osteology*, Academic Press, London, 2000.

Scheuer, L. and S. Black, *The Juvenile Skeleton*, Academic Press, London, 2004.

Schmitt, S., Mass graves and the collection of forensic evidence: genocide, war crimes, and crimes against humanity, in *Advances in Forensic Taphonomy: Method, Theory, and Archaeological Perspectives*, W.D. Haglund, and M.H. Sorg, Eds., CRC Press, Boca Raton, FL, 2002, pp. 277–292.

Schonstedt Instrument Company, *Instruction Manual: Model GA-52Cx*, Schonstedt Instrument Company, USA, 2001.

Schultz, J.J., Detecting Buried Remains Using Ground Penetrating Radar, Ph.D. Dissertation. University of Florida, Gainesville, 2003.

Schultz, J.J., A.B. Falsetti, M.E. Collins, S.K. Koppenjan, and M.W. Warren, The detection of forensic burials in Florida using GPR, *Proceedings of SPIE*, 4758:443–448, 2002.

Schwartz, J., *Skeleton Keys: An Introduction to Human Skeletal Morphology, Development, and Analysis*, Oxford University Press, London, 1995.

Scott D.D. and M. Connor, Context delecti: archaeological context in forensic work, in *Forensic Taphonomy: The Postmortem Fate of Human Remains*, W.H. Haglund and M.H. Sorg, Eds., CRC Press, Boca Raton, FL, 1997, pp. 27–38.

Sharer, R.J. and W. Ashmore, *Archaeology: Discovering Our Past*, 3rd ed., McGraw-Hill, New York, 2003.

Shih, D.G. and J.A. Doolittle, Using radar to investigate organic soil thickness in the Florida everglades, *Soil Science Society of America Journal*, 48:651–656, 1984.

Sigler-Eisenberg, B., Forensic research: expanding the concept of applied archaeology, *American Antiquity*, 50:650–655, 1985.

Simmons, T., Taphonomy of a Karstic cave execution site at Hrgar, Bosnia-Herzegovina, in *Advances in Forensic Taphonomy: Method, Theory, and Archaeological Perspectives*, W.D. Haglund and M.H. Sorg, Eds., CRC Press, Boca Raton, FL, 2002, pp. 263–276.

Skinner, M.F., D. Alempijevic, and M. Djuric-Srejic, Guidelines for international forensic bio-archaeology monitors of mass grave exhumations, *Forensic Science International*, 134:81–92, 2003.

Skinner, M. and R.A. Lazenby, *Found! Human Remains: A Field Manual for the Recovery of the Recent Human Skeleton*, Archaeology Press, Simon Fraser University, Burnaby, B.C., 1983.

Skinner, M., H.P. York, and M.A. Connor, Postburial disturbance of graves in Bosnia-Herzegovina, in *Advances in Forensic Taphonomy: Method, Theory, and Archaeological Perspectives*, W.D. Haglund and M.H. Sorg, Eds., CRC Press, Boca Raton, FL, 2002, pp. 293–308.

Smith, C., *A Manual of Forensic Entomology*, Cornell University Press, Ithaca, NY, 1995.

Snow, C.C., Forensic Anthropology, *Annual Reviews of Anthropology*, 11: 97–131, 1982.

Spennemann, D.H.R. and B. Franke, Archaeological techniques for exhumation: a unique data source for crime scene investigations, *Forensic Science International*, 74:5–15, 1995.

Steele, D.G. and C.A. Bramblett, *Anatomy & Biology of the Human Skeleton*, Texas A&M University Press, College Station, TX, 1988.

Sternberg, B.K. and J.W. McGill, Archaeology studies in southern Arizona using ground penetrating radar, *Journal of Applied Geophysics*, 33:209–225, 1995.

Stover, E. and M. Ryan, Baking bread with the dead, *Historical Archaeology*, 35(1):7–25, 2001.

Tz'u, S., *The Washing Away of Wrongs* (translated by B. McKnight), University of Michigan Press, MI, 1981.

Ubelaker, D.H., *Human Skeletal Remains: Excavation, Analysis, Interpretation*, Taraxcum, Washington, DC, 1989.

Ubelaker, D. and H. Scammell, *Bones: A Forensic Detective's Casebook*, HarperCollins, New York, 2000.

Van Sickle, J., *Basic GIS Coordinates*, CRC Press, Boca Raton, FL, 2004.

Vaughn, C.J., Ground-penetrating radar surveys used in archaeological investigations. *Geophysics*, 51:595–604, 1986.

Weedn, V.W., DNA identification, in *Forensic Dentistry*, P.G. Stimson and C.A. Mertz, Eds., CRC Press, Boca Raton, FL, 1997, pp. 37–46.

White, T.D., *Human Osteology*, 2nd ed., Academic Press, London, 2000.

Willey, P. and A. Heilman, Estimating time since death using plant roots and stems, *Journal of Forensic Sciences*, 32(5):1264–1270, 1987.

Wolf, D.J., Forensic anthropology scene investigations, in *Forensic Osteology: Advances in the Identification of Human Remains*, K. Reichs, Ed., Charles C. Thomas, Springfield IL, 1986, pp. 3–23.

Index

A

B